Movie Confidential

MOVIE
Confid

ential

Stories of sex, scandal, murder,
and mayhem in the Film Industry by

ANDREW SCHANIE

Printed in the United States of America
Distributed by Publishers Group West
First edition, first printing

CLERISY PRESS
PO Box 8874
Cincinnati, OH 45208-0874
www.clerisypress.com

ISBN 978-1-57860-354-1

Edited by
DONNA POEHNER

Cover and interior designed by
STEPHEN SULLIVAN

Layout by
SANDY KENT

Front and back cover photos appear courtesy of Photofest (Judy Garland), Library of Congress Prints and Photographs Division (Marlon Brando), Wikimedia Commons (Charlie Sheen, Drew Barrymore, Brad Pitt, Jean Harlow, Leonardo DiCaprio, Kate Winslet, Carole Lombard)

Photos in *Movie Confidential* appear courtesy of:
Photofest: pp. 48, 87, 134
Library of Congress Prints and Photographs Division: pp. 2, 7, 9, 27, 72, 110 (*Titanic*), 148, 172, 158, 167, 178, 210, 256
Wikimedia Commons: pp. 31, 37, 58, 62, 63, 66–67, 71, 72, 79, 80, 88, 100, 110 (Leonardo DiCaprio and Kate Winslet), 152, 164, 188, 192–193, 194, 197, 198, 208, 214–215, 217, 220, 223, 227, 238, 245, 249, 256
Other photos: p. 116, courtesy of the author; p. 199, courtesy of PETA

*For all my friends and family
who are still willing to talk to me.*

*Mainly for Chandra—
after all the years, you still laugh at my jokes.
You're my favorite person to have adventures with,
and you smell nice. Really nice.*

*Oh—and my dogs. They give me inspiration
in their own odd way.*

Table of

The Scoop: Tales of Lust, Legends, Weirdness, and Woe

CONTENTS

No Sequels: Brief Stories of Actors Who No Longer Need Agents

Table of

Missteps and Mistakes: Movieland's Embarrassments, Failures, Feuds, Fights, Stalkers, and Prostitutes

CONTENTS

THE SCOOP:

TALES

of Lust, Legends, Weirdness, and Woe

ROSCOE

"FATTY"

ARBUCKLE

Life of the

Party

1

Fatty Arbuckle Suffers a Crushing Victory

ഇ‍ൽ

ROSCOE CONKLING ARBUCKLE CAME crashing into the world on March 24, 1887, weighing sixteen pounds. If the birth of a sixteen-pound baby wasn't enough cause for alarm, it happened in the midst of a tornado. In Arbuckle's words, "My birth and a cyclone blew Smith Center [Kansas] off the map." He was the youngest of nine children—little wonder his mother stopped with Roscoe. His young life was not filled with happiness. Roscoe's mother died when he was twelve years old. His father was a drunk with a violent temper. But Roscoe grew up to be a rotund man who could make people laugh.

Roscoe "Fatty" Arbuckle may have played an idiot onscreen, but in reality he was an actor with great comic timing. His films were often a mixture of vulgarity and innocence— like a fat, horny five-year-old getting his first peck on the cheek.

Arbuckle could have been a legend. At one point he was more popular than his associate Charles Chaplin. He helped Buster Keaton become the star that he was. But one event at a Labor Day party—leading to the mysterious death of a young woman—would bring notoriety to Roscoe "Fatty" Arbuckle and ruin everything for him. Even after three trials—all ending in acquittal for Arbuckle—he would never recover from his transformation from a comedian into a laughingstock.

According to the book, *The Fatty Arbuckle Case* by Leo Guild, director Henry Lehrman had a new picture on the horizon starring Roscoe "Fatty" Arbuckle. It was on the set of this movie that Arbuckle met the young starlet Virginia Rappe for the first time. Rappe was involed with Henry Lehrman, but Arbuckle was infatuated with Virginia's beauty nonetheless and had no problem letting her know. But Virginia had no interest in being Arbuckle's girl. Although Arbuckle may have been a large man, he had a way of charming women. He wasn't a desperate man pining after something he couldn't have. He was a man who wore his emotions on his sleeve and left his options open. Should Virginia Rappe become single, he would swoop in to work his magic.

On Labor Day weekend in 1921, the planets aligned for disaster. Rappe had an argument with Lehrman, who left town on business after the argument, leaving the status of their relationship unknown. Arbuckle was aware of the rift and also was hosting a party at the St. Francis Hotel in San Francisco that weekend. He had booked three connecting rooms for the bash. Virginia would be one of the guests.

Over thirty guests attended the party, and there were various reports of what happened. Some say Virginia was drunk to the point of being sick. Others remembered her only having two, maybe three drinks. Regardless of how drunk she was or was not, at one point she needed to use the bathroom. Arbuckle offered to let her use the one that connected to his bedroom. She accepted and took his hand while he walked her there. Arbuckle also said loudly, as to address the room, "I've waited five years for you and now I've got you!" They entered the bedroom with no struggle; the door shut and then locked.

The party was in full swing. Arbuckle and Rappe were locked in seclusion. A tenant on the same floor called the front desk to complain about the noise. The phone in Arubuckle's suite rang; it was the front desk asking if the raging party could rage a little more quietly. Then, depending on the witness, a blood-curdling scream erupted from the bedroom. Arbuckle could be heard moaning loudly. Rappe shouted either, "He's killing me!" or "Don't kill me!" One of the guests, Maude Delmont, began pounding the door with her shoe, shouting for Arbuckle to leave Rappe alone.

Another call was placed to the front desk—this time from inside Arbuckle's suite. The manager arrived within minutes. He knocked hard on the bedroom door, demanding it be opened. The door was opened to reveal Arbuckle partially clothed and dripping with sweat. Rappe, who lay on the bed, appeared to be in immense pain. Again, depending on the witness, Virginia Rappe was nude, wearing some clothes, or had her clothes torn from her. A doctor was phoned in, who diagnosed the young woman as suffering from alcohol poisoning. The remedy . . . let her sleep it off. Arbuckle wanted the girl out of his bed. A different room in the hotel was booked for her to recover in. Arbuckle added the charge to his bill.

Rappe was moved to another room where two partygoers,

BUSTER KEATON IN "THE GENERAL"   5106-15

Fatty Arbuckle helped Buster Keaton become a star.

Maude Delmont and Zey Prevon, kept a vigil at her bedside. Rappe was not getting better. In fact, she was getting worse. Delmont called a second doctor who called for an ambulance. Virginia Rappe had suffered internal injuries. Her bladder had been ripped. She was transferred to Wakefield Sanatorium and underwent emergency surgery.

Only two people know for certain what happened behind the locked doors of that bedroom. One died four days later. The other was the primary suspect. Unsurprisingly vulgar rumors of what could have happened were floating around. Arbuckle raped her. He raped her twice; the second time caused internal damage. He violated the unconscious woman with a bottle. He violated her with a large piece of ice. Lots of ideas but no smoking gun.

Before Virginia died she was in and out of consciousness, running a high fever. A day nurse named Jeanne Jamison said

"He's killing me!"

that during a moment of consciousness the patient told her, "Arbuckle did it. Don't let him get away with it." Virginia Rappe died September 9, 1921, after peritonitis (an inflammation of the membrane that forms the lining of the abdominal cavity) had set in.

When reporters heard movie actress Virginia Rappe had died, they followed the trail that lead to Maude Delmont, who held back nothing. She told reporters of the party, the locked bedroom, the scream, and the man who had been alone with Virginia. Arbuckle was clueless about the events unfolding and continued with his Labor Day plans to take a trip with friends. When he returned home he found the authorities at his front door. They were there to question him about a suspicious death. Arbuckle phoned his attorney who told the funny man to keep

Virginia Rappe, the young actress whose mysterious death led to the demise of Fatty Arbuckle's career.

his mouth shut. Arbuckle had already told the lawmen that he had never been alone with the girl.

Arbuckle voluntarily went to the police station. He answered questions, provided a written statement, then later turned himself in to be arrested. Arbuckle and his lawyer anticipated a large bail, which they'd pay, and then they would fight and beat the charges. What neither Arbuckle nor his attorney expected to hear were the words "murder" and "no bail." Arbuckle went straight to jail. His hired legal help told him not to worry, this would get fixed.

Arbuckle's arrest launched Hollywood's first scandal. It threatened to consume not just Fatty Arbuckle, but the entire film industry. The morals of actors and filmmakers were called into question. Groups set out to put an end to what they perceived to be the modern-day Sodom and Gomorra. Several of Arbuckle's movies were either already in theaters or preparing for release. As the news exploded, almost all theaters declined to screen any more of Arbuckle's pictures. They reasoned that it was better to see how the trial played out and avoid the wrath of moral groups.

Self-imposed censorship would not be the only fallout from Arbuckle's arrest. Studios began inserting a morality clause into actors' contracts. It would be this morality clause that would later threaten the careers of Clark Gable and Joan Crawford when their private affair almost turned public. It wasn't about Hollywood wanting to be moral: it was about putting on the air of trying to do the right thing. Studios were aware of the troublesome activities their employees engaged in. As long as it stayed out of the paper, and the artist could still perform, no one cared.

Arbuckle stood firm—he had done nothing wrong. During the pretrial his attorney said, "When a man steals, he sets out to break the law. When a man drives drunk, he is in the process of breaking the law. But Roscoe Arbuckle set out to do no more than have sexual relations with a girl he had known for five years. I'd guess that a million men set out every night to try and do the same thing Arbuckle did, cohabitate with a woman." Witnesses and evidence were paraded in front of the grand jury. Most of it was bad news for the defendant. A dress with torn lace belonging to the victim was retrieved from Maude Delmont's trash can. Delmont had also changed part of her statement, saying that Arbuckle had "dragged" Rappe into the bedroom. Until then it had been asserted that Arbuckle held Rappe's hand when they walked into the bedroom together. However, Delmont also admitted, "I had at least ten drinks. I was drunk but I knew what I was doing. I might have acted foolishly but I was aware of it." Followed by, "I didn't exactly see Virginia and Arbuckle go into the bedroom, but I saw him drag her to the door. No, she did not make an outcry." When asked what she did when the first doctor examined Rappe, Delmont replied, "I and the detective went around and drank all the gin and orange juice that was left in the glasses." What to believe?

Other witnesses included Virginia's boyfriend, Henry Lehrman, who testified, "I loved her very much. You know we were engaged. You know Arbuckle was an ignorant man. He had too much money and too much success. Now I hope the law punishes him." Lehrman did not attend Rappe's funeral, saying that he was "advised not to" but would not say who had advised him. Lehrman did send tiger lilies and proceeded to marry a different woman six months later. Arbuckle's estranged wife, Minta Durfee, also chimed in, "I believe Roscoe is innocent. If they want me, I'll go to the trial." When asked about her opinion of Henry Lehrman, Durfee replied, "[He's] tasteless and a climber," and "He would never have married Miss Rappe, and he's putting on a big show for all the publicity he can get out of it."

Critics of Arbuckle would point out his mother's grave was still unmarked despite all his fortunes. If he cared so little about paying proper respect for his own mother, why would he respect any other woman? Nora Arbuckle, Roscoe's sister, told reporters that her brother was a kind person, and she knew he was innocent. Actor Rudolf Valentino said he'd always known Arbuckle to be a gentleman.

Prosecutors wanted murder in the first degree but the charges were reduced to manslaughter. Arbuckle could return home while he waited for the trial to begin. It was a small victory for the defense. The district attorney's office, on the other hand, was outraged. They felt Arbuckle's people had used money and intimidation in getting the charges reduced. Nurse Vera Cumberland claimed she was threatened and told not to testify. Zey Prevon changed the story she had originally told police. Now she

I have never done anything

claimed Arbuckle was a good guy, and she really didn't see much at the party. Prosecutors felt she had been paid off and put their star witnesses under twenty-four-hour watch.

The first trial began. The defense called Betty Campbell, who had been at the party. During her testimony she said, "Fatty is not guilty. I am sure of it. During the party when I asked him where Virginia was, he said she wasn't feeling well and he had sent her to the bedroom down the hall." And, "He cared. It seems to me Virginia Rappe wasn't feeling well even before she went into the bedroom."

A strong witness for prosecution during the pretrial, Maude Delmont, was not called to the stand. Delmont was now facing legal woes of her own, as she was found to be a bigamist. Also, Delmont was known as "Madame Black": she used girls by having them show up at parties and then claim a producer or director tried to rape them. They would use the allegations to extort money. The prosecution feared this would discredit her as a witness, so she stayed off the stand.

The prosecution brought in doctors who treated Rappe at the sanatorium to testify. It was their opinion that external force (rape) killed Rappe, not disease.

The defense opened their argument with claims Arbuckle was alone with Rappe for less than ten minutes. Anyone could have opened the door if there was trouble because Arbuckle never locked the door. Hotel detective George Glennon, the same detective Maude Delmont claimed she finished all the drinks with, gave his testimony, "Miss Rappe was in great pain. She was clutching at her abdomen and tearing at her clothes. I asked her if Arbuckle or anyone else had hurt her. She was indignant and

that I am ashamed of.

swore no one had anything to do with it. She said Arbuckle had only been kind to her."

Whenever possible the defense asked the same question, "Was Virginia Rappe drunk during the party?" The answer was always yes. One witness, Fred Fishbeck, replied, "Very."

The original doctor to see Virginia Rappe at the St. Francis Hotel testified she had no bruises on her body when he examined her. Under oath he told the jury, "She constantly reiterated that she didn't remember any sequence of events or when or how the pain started." A former housekeeper also testified Rappe had "violent and threatening" spells of pain where she would tear at her clothes. Several more witnesses were called in who described Rappe going into spells of pain followed by tearing at her own clothes. These attacks were usually preceded by social or binge drinking. A valiant effort was being made to show the young woman's death as a pre-existing condition.

Physical evidence was introduced. The prosecution claimed smeared fingerprints on a door proved Rappe fought to escape the bedroom. The defense called in a maid who said she had cleaned the suite, including the door in question. The fingerprints, the defense contended, could have belonged to anyone.

What everyone was waiting for finally happened. Roscoe Arbuckle took the stand to testify in his defense. His story was that he was merely trying to enjoy breakfast with friends when visitors descended onto his hotel room. He had intended to take a friend out for a ride in his car. When he went into his bathroom, he found Virginia on the floor. Worried for her safety he placed her on the bed and then went back to taking care of business in the washroom. When he checked on Virginia ten minutes later, he found she had fallen off the bed, so he called for help. During cross-examination, the prosecution did everything they could to poke holes in his story. They said his testimony was the seventh version of what he claimed happened that night. They called him a sex-mad pervert who raped a woman he couldn't have. But Arbuckle stayed calm while answering questions and asserted that he was telling the whole truth when he recounted the series of events that took place that Labor Day weekend.

The jury began their deliberations. The first collection of ballots showed a count of eleven to one to acquit Arbuckle. The lone holdout was a woman who said she would continue to vote guilty until hell froze over. The final ballot tally still showed in favor of acquitting Arbuckle by ten to two. The presiding judge declared the jury hopelessly hung. There would be a second trial. Finding an impartial jury for a second trial was going to be difficult considering the heavy press coverage and sensational headlines during the first one.

Roscoe Arbuckle addressed the journalists and gave the following statement, "I wasn't legally acquitted but I was morally acquitted. I am not guilty. I only tried to help Miss Rappe. I have never done anything that I am ashamed of. I have only tried all my life to give joy and happiness to the world. I hope the public will have faith in me and let me prove myself all over again."

Arbuckle was allowed to prove himself all over again. The second trial began introducing all the same scenarios and evidence again. The biggest surprise for the second trial was the amended testimony of Zey Prevon, who initially said Rappe told her, "He hurt me." This time Zey took the stand and said, "In the first trial I said I heard Virginia Rappe say, 'I'm dying, I'm dying. He hurt me.' That wasn't entirely true. I did hear Virginia say, 'I'm dying, I'm dying.' I didn't hear her say, 'He hurt me' or anything like that." Zey Prevon continued, "Now you want to know why I lied? Well, Mr. Brady tried to force me to sign that little bit about 'He hurt me.' I didn't want to. They locked me in a cell and said I'd never come out until I signed the statement." First Delmont, now Prevon—prosecutors were losing all their star witnesses. "I had visions of spending the rest of my life in jail," Prevon continued. "After I signed, they sent me home and guarded my house so I couldn't leave. The days of the trial, they had me in the District Attorney's office learning a script they had prepared for me."

Prevon was told charges of perjury would be brought against her but they never were.

For a second time a jury was sent off to determine the fate of Roscoe Arbuckle. After thirty hours of deliberation, the ballots read eight votes not guilty and four votes guilty. After another fourteen hours of deliberating, the jurors took the vote to ballot again. This time the tide had changed: only three still thought the funny man innocent, and nine now thought him guilty. After more deliberating, the vote still didn't change. Another hung jury was declared.

You would think after two mistrials the District Attorney's office would drop the charges. Their pool of witnesses was thinning out. The physical evidence didn't seem to prove anything except there were smudged fingerprints on the door. Twenty-four taxpayers could not come to consensus despite the time, resources, and money poured into the case. But prosecutors were determined to push on and requested a third trial. The request was granted.

The third time proved to be a charm for the comedian, who had visibly lost weight and seemed more serious. The defense made it a point to stress that Virginia Rappe was sick before she collapsed in Arbuckle's bedroom. Even her dentist was called in to testify Rappe was a "nervous" patient, who had suffered extreme lower-abdominal pain during a tooth extraction. Another doctor took the stand to say that while there were no documented cases of a woman's bladder rupturing during sex, there were numerous cases of men suffering heart attacks during the act of

The jury was dismissed to deliberate.

love. No one had yet to press murder or manslaughter charges against these women. The doctor declared it was an act of God where no one was to blame.

Zey Prevon would not testify this time. She had fled the country.

Prosecutors brought in a young woman who was engaged, aspired to be an actress, desired to have children, and happened to be the same age and size as Virginia Rappe. The reason? To show the jury what Rappe would have been like if she were still alive. While the move may have been big on sentiment, it did nothing to prove guilt.

Arbuckle's defense team had the stronger hand. During their closing argument, the name of every witness who testified that the victim had a pre-existing condition was repeated. Arbuckle's attorney emphasized his client's innocence by saying the prosecutors had no evidence of murder. No evidence of any object used on Miss Rappe. No witness to what happened to Miss Rappe. It was tragic, but tragedy did not make Roscoe Arbuckle a murderer. Arbuckle was painted as a man who used his talents to make people happy. His reward for his gift was unjust.

The jury was dismissed to deliberate. They returned six minutes later. Roscoe "Fatty" Arbuckle was found not guilty. The jury, along with two alternates, did not stop at just acquitting the man, they also issued an apology to him.

> Acquittal is not enough for Roscoe Arbuckle. We feel that a great injustice has been done him. We feel also that it was our only plain duty to give him this exoneration. There was not the slightest proof adduced

They returned **six** minutes later.

> to connect him in any way with the commission of a crime.
>
> He was manly throughout the case and told a straightforward story on the witness stand, which we all believed.
>
> The happening at the hotel was an unfortunate affair for which Arbuckle, so the evidence shows, was in no way responsible.
>
> We wish him success and hope that the American people will take the judgment of fourteen men and women who have sat listening for thirty-one days to the evidence that Roscoe Arbuckle is entirely innocent and free from all blame.

Arbuckle was found guilty of one crime: possession of alcohol during Prohibition. He paid the maximum fine allowable, $500. After the trial he had faced, they might as well have told him to sit in the corner.

He was a free man but his freedom came with a seven-hundred-thousand-dollar price made payable to his attorney. Arbuckle had lost his home and the car he loved. A jury found him innocent, but segments of the public felt he had gotten away with murder. Letters of complaint poured into the studio, and theaters that projected Arbuckle's movies had their screens damaged. Arbuckle was told public perception would have to cool down before he could star in pictures again.

Arbuckle found an ally during his career depression in a woman named Doris Deene. She became his second wife in 1925. Deene told Arbuckle he had a gift, and it would be a sin to waste it. Maybe he needed to come back as a different person, but he needed to come back. Arbuckle did come back, this time as a director using the pseudonym William Goodrich. He had talent behind the camera just as he did in front of it. Yet, when the true identity of "B. Good" was revealed, the complaints rolled in again.

Arbuckle traveled to the East Coast and performed in a play called *Baby Mine*. It was a hit, leaving Arbuckle to wonder if the tide was beginning to change. He began a stage tour that stopped dead in its tracks in Minneapolis. The protestors came out again, and his show was canceled. The rejection was huge. Arbuckle's drinking became heavier. He divorced his wife and was arrested several more times, usually for speeding or partying.

Another attempt for a comeback was made when Arbuckle opened the Plantation Club in Hollywood. No one protested the comic performing in his own club. Business was even profitable . . . until the stock market crash. The doors to the Plantation Club closed.

Arbuckle was married for a third time to an actress named Adie McPhail. His love life was getting another chance, as was his movie career when Jack Warner approached him to start working in two-reel comedies again. Warner Brothers studios would even let Arbuckle work under his real name. The films were a success, and on June 29, 1933, Roscoe "Fatty" Arbuckle signed a contract to make a feature-length movie. Arbuckle said it was the happiest day of his life. It was also his last. Roscoe Arbuckle died of a heart attack that very night.

A script for a film about Arbuckle's life exists. Over the years, a variety of actors have been associated with playing the role of Fatty: John Belushi, John Candy, Chris Farley, standup comedian Jim Gaffigan, and *Jackass* stunt person Preston Lacy. However, filming never began with any of the proposed leads, and the project is said to be shelved. Fatty just can't win.

CLARK GABLE

Ready, Willing, and Gable

2

Gable Loves Older Women. Gable Also Loves Married Ladies. Hitler Loves Gable. Dillinger Wouldn't Miss It.

ഓ൝

DURING THE HISTORY OF THE WORLD THERE have been two men who could wear the pencil mustache without being thought of as creepy kid touchers. One being the infamous Baltimore director John Waters, who is also known as the Pope of Trash. The other is Clark Gable, who was also known as the King of Hollywood. But before Clark Gable could be King, a womanizer, or even grow a mustache, he had a long road with many obstacles to overcome.

On February 1, 1901, William Clark Gable was born at home in a small coal mining town in Ohio. Ten months later his mother died. Clark's father, Will Gable, was said to be a womanizer and a heavy drinker. Will Gable eventually remarried. His bride, Jennie Gable, was introduced to young Clark as his stepmother. Clark would be her only child, and she spoiled him constantly.

While Clark Gable was finishing up grade school, World War I was erupting. When Gable was a teen, the war was still raging on. Gable paid his father $175 for his Ford and moved to Akron, Ohio, to work in the factories. At seventeen he saw the stage play *The Bird of Paradise* and was so taken by the story and the actors that he finagled his way into working behind the scenes

Clark Gable was twenty-three years old. Josephine Dillon was forty-one.

and eventually got his first taste of the stage with one line, "Your cab is here, madam." That one line was all it took to hook young Gable.

Although Gable wanted to stay in Akron, his father persuaded him to move out West to work on the oil fields. At age twenty-one, Clark Gable left the business of drilling for black gold permanently. He spent time working with traveling theaters and performed physical labor when the theater troops didn't pan out. During this time, Gable was introduced to the woman who would be his first wife, Josephine Dillon, an acting coach. She was able to bring out his strength and abilities, making him a full-fledged actor.

Gable and Dillon moved to Los Angeles together to chase their acting dream. In December of 1924, they married. Clark Gable was twenty-three years old. Josephine Dillon was forty-one.

In his early Hollywood years, Gable mainly appeared as an extra in silent movies and worked his way into more prominent roles in live theater. During one of his tours with live theater, Gable began an affair with a wealthy actress named Pauline Frederick. Like Gable's wife, Frederick was much older than he was—eighteen years older. Though his wife seemed willing to look the other way, Gable moved out of their home. This would be the beginning of the end for their marriage.

Gable continued to tour and struck up another affair with an older woman, Ria Langham, a wealthy widow who was seventeen years older than Gable. Langham felt Gable had what it takes to be famous and offered to support him in New York City with the stipulation that he marry her. One problem: Clark Gable's current wife wasn't ready to let go, and to prove her support and love for her husband, she made a bee line to the big city to track down roles. Using this to his advantage, the future King of Hollywood didn't bother giving Josephine Dillon the final boot until he was situated.

Ria Langham was seventeen

With Dillon out of the picture, Ria Langham moved to New York to be with her man. She kept her word by buying him expensive clothes and paying his bills to live in expensive apartments. Gable attempted to keep his end of the bargain, but Dillon stretched out the divorce for as long as possible . . . can't really blame her.

With Dillon finally out of the picture, Gable and Langham claimed to have married on March 31, 1930. The legitimacy of their nuptials would eventually be scrutinized, but we'll get to that in a minute. Though Gable was in a committed relationship—if not already married—that didn't stop him from romancing his female costars.

Gable continued acting in live productions as he made his way back to California. It didn't hurt to have sugar mama Ria Langham on his side. Once in California, a new talent agent was hired, and motion picture work finally began to drizzle in. His earliest work was as an extra or very minor roles. Nonetheless, he had his foot in the door, appearing in movies like *The Painted Desert*, *The Easiest Way*, *The Finger Points*, and *Night Nurse* (all filmed in 1931).

With his relentless grab for the golden ring, Gable convinced MGM he was a capable actor. MGM signed Gable to a year contract for $650 a week. If studio bosses decided they liked what they saw, his contract would be renewed with a pay increase at the end of the year. Little did anyone know he would out perform all expectations and grow into a movie star big enough to match his physique.

Critics began to take notice, commenting on his magnetic personality and solid acting ability. Work was picking up and parts were getting bigger. By the end of 1931 he would also act

years older than Gable.

in *Dance, Fools, Dance*, *The Secret Six*, and *A Free Soul* among others. All the hard work, hard living, and occasional shady maneuver had paid off. Clark Gable got his first starring role in a motion picture. He landed the lead in *Sporting Blood*.

Around this time Gable's second wife, Ria Langham, began voicing her displeasure with her "husband," rising star Clark Gable. She was suspicious of his relationships with various women and rightfully so. It's not like the man was single when she started dating him. She also began talking about how she and Gable weren't actually married. The studio had no desire to be involved in the scandal, and Gable didn't want to lose his studio contract. To make everyone happy, an appointment was made in a judge's chamber where the two said/resaid their vows.

Gable went back to working on *Susan Lenox: Her Fall and Rise* and *Possessed* (both 1931). Ria went on as Mrs. Clark Gable. While shooting *Possessed*, Gable began a love affair with Joan Crawford. In Warren G. Harris's biography of *Clark Gable*, he quotes Crawford as saying, "In the picture, Clark and I were madly in love. When the scenes ended, the emotion didn't." To add fuel to the fire of forbidden love, Gable and Crawford were both married. Again the studio feared scandal, and future projects with the two actors working together were axed. Filming for *Possessed* wrapped, and Gable kept on working without missing a beat, appearing in *Hell Divers* (1931) and *Polly of the Circus* (1932).

Not caring or having not learned his lesson, Gable began an affair with his *Polly of the Circus* costar, Marion Davies, who was also married. During the affair with Davies, Gable's contract came up for renewal. Through contacts, Davies was able to raise Gable's pay to $1,500 a week.

Gable continued to have many affairs that he attempted to keep secret. Billy Grad, an MGM executive, said of Gable, "He'd screw anything. A girl didn't have to be pretty or even clean." Gable spent 1933 working on *The White Sister, Hold Your Man, Night Flight,* and *Dancing Lady. Dancing Lady* would be the first time Gable and Crawford worked together since their adulterous relationship almost went public while filming *Possessed. Dancing Lady* was anything but a good time for Gable, who missed weeks of shooting due to illness and Crawford ending their liaison to take up with a different costar.

Always looking forward, Gable recovered and began work on *It Happened One Night* (1934). Initially Gable wanted nothing to do with the project, but it ultimately led to a big surprise and an even bigger boost to his career. From there, Gable went on to star in *Men in White* (1934) where he again romanced his costar. This time it was Elizabeth Allen, who was already well known in her homeland, Great Britain. And in case you were wondering—she was married.

Time rolled on and Gable moved to his next project, playing a thug named Blackie Gallagher in *Manhattan Melodrama* (1934). Catapulting *Manhattan Melodrama* from Hollywood

Bank robber John Dillinger was a huge fan of Clark Gable.

blockbuster into the realm of pop culture was a man named John Dillinger: The man who went on bank robbing sprees and landed a slot on the most wanted list was a huge Clark Gable fan. He never missed one of Gable's movies even if it meant he had to risk being captured. It turns out the risk was greater than Dillinger had imagined, and authorities gunned him down after he left a screening of *Manhattan Melodrama*.

In Clark Gable's next movie, *Chained*, he would costar with Joan Crawford again. While filming, the two rekindled their affair except this time it was casual and purely physical. *Chained* was well received, and the studio placed them together again in *Forsaking All Others*. Gable moved on to work on *Call of the*

If he saw something he wanted, he went after it.

Wild, where once again he struck up an affair with costar Loretta Young. Sure, he was still romancing Elizabeth Allen, just finished with Joan Crawford (again), and ignoring his second wife, the independently wealthy Ria Langham. But Clark Gable had fame now, and if he saw something he wanted, he went after it.

During all this work and bedding, Gable was notified he was nominated for an Academy Award. It was a best actor nomination for his role in *It Happened One Night*. Gable attended the Academy Awards and collected his statue. As a result of this win, his pay rose from $2,000 to $4,000 a week. Pay increase and award in hand, Gable went to work on *Mutiny on the Bounty*, where he argued nonstop with some actors and partied wildly with others.

After the premier of *Mutiny on the Bounty*, Gable moved out of the house he shared with Langham, who told reporters no other woman was involved. This was a half truth since *mul-*

tiple women were involved. Not wanting to lose half of what he had worked for, Clark Gable held off on getting divorced and instead opted to pay Langham a monthly fee for living expenses. Gable would go on making movies and sleeping with starlets. Ria would go on getting to enjoy the perks of being married to a movie star.

Clark Gable then received his second best actor Academy Award nomination—this time for *Mutiny on the Bounty*. Gable attended the ceremony, taking as his date Merle Oberon, who received a best actress nomination for *The Dark Angel*. Gable did not win an Oscar that year. Neither did his date.

Around this time Gable began pursuing an actress named Carole Lombard. Initially Lombard had no interest in Gable outside of friendship. Her rejections to his advances made Gable crazy. Her penchant for practical jokes, like releasing two doves in his apartment as a peace offering after an argument, made him crazier. Once, as a payback gag, Gable gave her a live cougar cub when she asked him to bring her back a wildcat from one of his hunting trips. Their flirting and pursuit of the heart was a cat-and-mouse game usually reserved for the movies.

It was clear why Clark Gable lusted after Carole Lombard. She was a blonde firecracker with the ability to swear a serious blue streak. She took her acting very seriously and enjoyed

"He'd screw **anything**. A girl didn't have to be pretty or even clean.

sports. She was eight years younger than Gable and would eventually become his wife. It would be the third marriage for Gable and the second for Lombard.

In the meantime Gable found himself in such high demand he began working in Radio Theater. The work was easier than movies or stage acting, and he was able to up his pay again to $6,500. Gable had no intention of leaving the movies behind. This was simply a side business. And why not take the money if it's easy?

Back at MGM studios Gable was teaming up with Joan Crawford yet again in *Love on the Run*. Crawford's career was in a serious slump, and the studio saw appearing with Gable as the only way to pull her back out. *Love on the Run* would also costar Crawford's real-life husband, Franchot Tone. Gable and Tone had previously worked together on *Mutiny on the Bounty* and got along well. It would be Tone and Crawford, the husband and wife, who would cause the tension. Tone was frustrated over being cast as a supporting actor to his wife . . . again.

She was a blonde firecracker with the ability to swear a serious blue streak.

Gable's affair with Carole Lombard grew more serious. His other affairs soon dried up and died. Gable's wife Ria, no longer happy being a wife in name only, began collecting what she need-ed for a divorce. The Gable/Lombard love connection had been receiving press attention, and Ria couldn't take it any more.

If Clark Gable needed any more trouble it came in the form of a forty-seven-year-old Essex woman named Violet Nor-ton. Norton had hired a private detective who showed up at the gates of MGM studios. The private dick also came with a story that Gable had impregnated Norton in 1922 while using the alias Frank Billings. As author David Brent points out in his book, *Clark Gable*, "Clark had not been issued with a passport

Carole Lombard, Gable's third wife, was the love of his life.

until 1930," and "[additionally] he had never been to England." The case went to trial by jury, and Gable's former lover, Franz Dorfler, testified Gable was living on her parents' farm during 1922–1923, making it impossible for him to have fathered a child in another country. The jury found Gable innocent, and the accuser, Violet Norton, was deported. Perhaps Clark Gable coined the term "Eurotrash."

What no one knew was that Clark Gable *did* father a child outside of his marriage. His affair with actress Loretta Young produced a daughter, who Gable visited just once. With no father or husband in the picture, Loretta Young traveled to San Francisco and put the child up for adoption. Young would later adopt her own child, hiding the truth from everyone. When the child grew older and asked where her father was, Young told her he was dead.

Clark Gable was a man's man.

The love triangle between Ria Gable, Clark Gable, and Carole Lombard was in full swing. Gable would have divorced Ria Gable earlier to make Lombard his wife but he detested the idea of losing money in a divorce settlement. Then, while *Gone With the Wind* was in preproduction, a tabloid ran an article on all three of them. MGM was once again stuck in the middle of a Clark Gable love affair, but this time religious groups were writing complaint letters in response to the article. Carole Lombard was a free agent in the studio system. Gable, on the other hand, was bound by his contract. He was given the option to divorce Ria Gable and marry Lombard or end his relationship with the young actress.

In the early part of 1939 the divorce between Ria and Clark Gable was finalized. He would pay half his current pension, and she would agree to not slow down the process—though the idea of causing her now ex-husband unnecessary complications pleased her. During a brief break in filming *Gone With the Wind*, Gable and Lombard eloped, telling no one until after the fact. The two were ecstatic. They truly seemed to be soul mates.

Even though the two loved each other deeply, Clark Gable would again be unfaithful. Lombard was aware Gable still carried on sexual relations with other women. She acknowledged she couldn't stop him if she wanted to. So as long as his extramarital affairs were only physical, she allowed it.

In the midst of all the marriage drama, *Gone With the Wind* began preproduction in 1938. The Civil War period novel, written by Margaret Mitchell, was a smash hit and stayed on the best-seller lists for three-and-a-half years. The studios wanted Gable to play Rhett Butler. The fans wanted to see Gable play Rhett Butler. Gable had no interest in playing Rhett Butler. He almost passed on the movie entirely—the movie that continued to make him a movie star for generations after his death. What made Gable decide to act in *Gone With the Wind* was simple: money. He was given a bonus of $50,000 on top of his going contract rate.

During the early stages of filming, Gable was having a hard time on the set. He felt the character of Rhett Butler did not fit the mold of characters he was used to playing. Characters that made him famous. Clark Gable was a man's man. Women pursued him. He didn't pursue women. Clark Gable didn't cry, but Rhett Butler did. Tensions were also high between Gable and director George Cukor. The studio intervened and removed Cukor from the job, replacing him with *Wizard of Oz* director Victor Fleming. Gossip began to circulate Gable was a homophobe and had the homosexual director fired. Later the gossip mutated into Clark Gable being a homosexual. After a brief regrouping, production on *Gone With the Wind* resumed. The tension eased, and Gable became more comfortable with his part.

Come Oscar time, Gable was nominated for best actor but would lose to Robert Donat for his role in *Goodbye, Mr. Chips*. Hattie McDaniel who played Mammy was nominated and won best supporting actress. McDaniel was the first African American to be nominated for an Academy Award. *Gone With the Wind* would also take home best picture, beating out *The Wizard of Oz*. Victor Fleming, who was also a director on *The Wizard of Oz*, won best director. By the end of the night, *Gone With the Wind* won a record of eight awards.

Though Gable did not walk away with a second golden statue, *Gone With the Wind* broke all box office records. As a result Gable's contract was renegotiated for an additional three years. His pay went up to $7,500 a week and would rise to $10,000 a week in the contract's final year.

Gable was **crushed**.

Earning more than ever, Gable went on to star in *Boom Town* and *Comrade X* (both 1940). Both films would feature Hedy Lamarr as Gable's love interest. Lamarr was a rising sexpot, and Carole Lombard was known to stop by the set to supervise shoots. Clark Gable had become so famous, and his pay so high, that he no longer needed to make movies back to back. In 1941 Gable appeared in only two films, *They Met in Bombay* and *Honky Tonk*.

The Gables had it all. They were famous, wealthy, and, for the most part, made their own work schedule. The couple had bought a small ranch and were enjoying the life of luxury. While not working, the biggest disturbance the husband and wife faced was the occasional fan who overstepped their boundaries. Then news arrived of the attack on Pearl Harbor. The U.S. would be entering World War II, and Lombard encouraged Gable to enlist.

Gable, while patriotic in spirit, had no intention of leaving his plush lifestyle. While Clark did not volunteer to fight in the war, the Gables did contribute in other ways: They entertained troops during their R&R breaks, donated money and even the use of their horses from the ranch. Lombard toured the United States selling war bonds. Her spirit energized audiences, and she sold more than double the amount of bonds anticipated.

On January 16, 1942, Clark Gable was preparing a glamorous welcome-home party for his wife, who would soon be back to the ranch from her tour of selling war bonds. Gable received a call: The plane in which Carole Lombard was traveling had collided with Double Up Peak just outside of Las Vegas. At first there was hope of finding survivors, but in the end, all the passengers had perished. After an investigation, the cause of the crash would be attributed to pilot error.

Gable was crushed. Friends said he never fully recovered, becoming more of a quiet and serious man. For her dedication and achievements for the war effort, a naval ship was named after Carole Lombard.

Gable took time off from shooting *Somewhere I'll Find You* to mourn. He lost weight. He spent most of his time on the ranch he shared his wife, reflecting on their life together. He ordered her belongings in the bedroom to remain the way she left them. He'd return to the set February 23. Until then they'd have to shoot around his scenes. Co-star Lana Turner later called Gable a "consummate professional" in reference to his ability and dedication during this tragic time.

The loneliness and loss became too much for the widower. He thought of his wife's words encouraging him to enlist. The United States Air Force would be getting a new recruit. The King of Hollywood was enlisting. While he believed in defending his country, it was clear he made the personal sacrifice in memory of his wife.

The media was buzzing with the news of Clark Gable entering the fight. MGM was worried about losing their biggest male star. Fans couldn't stop talking about it, including the leader of the German Nazi party, Adolph Hitler. When Hitler had heard Clark Gable was changing careers, he got his autograph book ready. Hitler was a huge film buff and a fan of *Gone With the Wind*. Gable was one of his favorite actors. A Nazi radio broadcast even sent out a message, "We'll be seeing you soon in Germany, Clark. You will be welcome there too." A German journalist went so far as to attempt to make a connection between Clark Gable and Joseph Goebbels. (Supposedly, the name "Gable" had previously been anglicized from "Goebel.")

While in the service, Clark Gable was an aerial gunner and also helped produce a combat film for the Office of War Information. Gable walked away from gunning and back to MGM a decorated war hero in 944. His contract was extended another seven years, obligating him to make two films a year. His return to the studio was celebrated but Gable played down the hero angle. To him the real heroes were still fighting.

Hitler never did get his autograph.

As a sign of respect Gable refused to make another movie until the war ended. He kept his promise by not stepping in front of the camera until thirteen days after victory was declared in Europe. What's that? The war was still going on in the Pacific? Oops.

Gable did go back to dating, and he dated many women including Dolly O'Brien, who was six years his senior. He was lonely but had no intentions of taking another bride. Because of the emotional tolls suffered, his drinking became out of control. He was behind the wheel of a very public and much gossiped-about one-car accident. During a hunting trip he was arrested for shooting more ducks than allowed. As hard as he tried, the women and booze weren't filling the hole left by Carole Lombard.

During World War II, some tried to make a connection between the names "Gable" and "Goebbels." Joseph Goebbels (above left) was a prominent figure in the Third Reich. It was rumored that Adolf Hitler loved Gable's movies.

Gable also continued to make movies, but as he was growing older, the critics were growing less kind. References to his jowls and leathery skin began popping up. Hemorrhoid cream was applied to his face, and the skin behind his ears was taped back in an attempt to make him look younger. His aging really stood out when he was teamed again with Loretta Young, the mother of his secret love child, in *Key to the City* (1950). Young still looked vivacious next to Gable, whose hard living showed on his face.

Gable needed companionship. Whether because of loneliness or love, he would marry two more times. First he married Sylvia Ashley, a socialite three years younger than Gable. Ashley was also a model and stage actress, who found her stardom fading due to her age. The fourth Mrs. Gable was horrible when it came to her husband's hobbies like camping, fishing, or hunting. She had no interest for it. Instead she preferred to spend money to maintain a lavish lifestyle. The two may have been great lovers but not ideal husband and wife. One year and five months into the marriage, Gable announced he wanted out, and Ashley filed for divorce.

Gable continued making movies to mixed reviews and uneven box office results. When it came time to renew his contract with MGM, he wanted a percentage of the profits for the movies he starred in. MGM balked at the idea, refusing to get involved in the profit sharing that many freelance actors enjoyed. As a result, Gable walked away from his twenty-three-year relationship with the studio to go freelance. He never worked with MGM again.

Gable still had a talent for wowing the ladies, never needing to be lonely. One of the more notable flings was with Grace Kelly, whom Gable began seeing while working on *Mogambo* together in 1953. Gable genuinely cared for Kelly and eventually

At twenty-eight years her senior, he

let her go, realizing that, at twenty-eight years her senior, he was too old for the saucy starlet.

Clark Gable met his fifth and final wife in Kay Williams, who was fifteen years younger than he was. Williams was a model and an actress who usually obtained small roles. Sparks did fly between the two lovers but not with the same intensity Gable shared with Lombard. Williams loved the outdoors and enjoyed accompanying her husband on hunting or fishing trips. Gable took her and her two children from a previous marriage into his home. He enjoyed the family life and cherished the company. Unlike the previous wife, Williams was not preoccupied with material things. Friends pointed out that Kay had a physical resemblance to Lombard. She could also belt out the blue language, and had a gift for trading barbs with her husband. Perhaps Gable was subconsciously trying to replace Carole Lombard with an imitation. But one thing was clear: Clark Gable loved Kay Williams and made her Kay Gable.

Professionally, Gable didn't just acknowledge his age, he often joked about it. He wanted to start making movies that better reflected his strong but aging persona. No longer was it appropriate to play romantic leads—especially when the love interest was twenty plus years younger. So, in 1960, Clark Gable signed on for what would be his final performance, playing an aging cowboy in *The Misfits*. He was paid $750,000 for the sixteen-week shoot (which went over schedule, creating additional pay for Gable) as well as profit sharing. It was his biggest check for making a single movie.

During filming, Kay Gable announced she was pregnant. Gable was ecstatic and made his own announcement. The King

was too old for the **saucy** starlet.

would retire after one more movie to become a full-time family man. Weeks after completing the most dangerous and physically demanding scenes, Clark Gable was hospitalized, suffering from coronary thrombosis. November 16, 1960, Gable was in the hospital recovering, when he suffered a massive heart attack and died. On the day of his funeral, all the Hollywood studios flew their flags at half-staff.

Kay Gable gave birth to John Clark Gable on March 20, 1961—four months after his father's death. For the second time, Clark Gable fathered a child who would never know him.

CHARLIE CHAPLIN

The Comedic

Red

Scare

3

Charlie Chaplin Gets the Tramp Stamp

ON SEPTEMBER 20, 1952, THE LONDON
Daily Mirror reported that silent-movie star Charlie Chaplin would be detained by immigration officials and "held until he was brought before a court of inquiry to decide if he could re-enter the country" should he attempt to cross the United States border. Chaplin had just finished working on his latest movie, *Limelight*, and was vacationing with his fourth wife when a wire message was delivered to him. Attorney General James McGranery was revoking Chaplin's ability to re-enter the United States.

Charlie Chaplin was no stranger to controversy. He had been married four times, fathering eleven children. The first wife was Mildred Harris, who was more than twelve years younger than Chaplin. They wed in 1918 when Harris was sixteen and Chaplin was twenty-nine. Their marriage produced one son named Norman Spencer Chaplin, who died three days after his birth. Just two years after the pair said "I do" they divorced. Harris went for Chaplin's money. Chaplin went for Harris's reputation, saying she had a lesbian affair.

There was an even greater age difference between wife number two and Charlie Chaplin. Lita Grey was sixteen when she married Chaplin, who was then thirty-five, in 1924. The union produced two sons—Charles Chaplin Jr. and Sydney Chaplin.

Many claim Chaplin's relationship with Grey is what turned his hair gray

Not only was the relationship a wreck, but Chaplin was facing troubles related to unpaid taxes. The marriage dissolved into a costly divorce in less than three years. Many claim Chaplin's relationship with Grey is what turned his hair gray.

Third in line was Paulette Goddard, who can be seen in starring roles alongside Chaplin in *Modern Times* and *The Great Dictator*. Goddard was twenty-four years younger than Chaplin, and they kept their marriage secret to not affect her acting career. The two wed in 1936 when Goddard was twenty-six and Chaplin was fifty. The couple bore no children and divorced six years later under what was described as mutual terms.

Chaplin married his fourth and final wife during an ongoing paternity case. The dispute began in 1943 and went well into 1944. A blood test proved Chaplin was not the father, but the court ruled for him to pay child support anyway. In the midst of the drama, Oona O'Neill became Oona Chaplin on June 16, 1943. Oona was eighteen and Chaplin was fifty-four. The thirty-six-year age difference was the largest of Chaplin's four marriages. The union provided eight more children for the Chaplin clan, five girls and three boys.

Now, what had started as a family vacation for the Chaplins had become an exile. In the book *Remembering Charlie*, Jerry Epstein, a friend and worker on *Limelight*, has quoted Chaplin as saying, "I could have never found success in England. This really is the land of opportunity." However, a different quote, this one appearing in an issue of the *Daily Worker* dated October,

"Thank God for communism."

25, 1942, gained the attention of the U.S. government. Charlie's quote in the paper read, "Thank God for communism. They say communism may spread all over the world. I say so what?" That same year, on October 14, Chaplin was the keynote speaker of the "Second Front" meeting held at Carnegie Hall. The event had a strong Hollywood support base that wanted to see troops diverted from the Pacific to Europe. They felt the larger numbers would crush Hitler's army, forcing them out of the Soviet Union. "Second Front" was sponsored by the "Artists' Front to Win the War," a group with numerous members in the communist party.

In 1947 Chaplin made a movie called *Monsieur Verdoux*, which he himself described as "cynical pessimism." It was the first time Charlie appeared on screen as a different character other than the Tramp. This time Charlie plays Monsieur Verdoux, a man who marries women, takes all their money, and then kills them in order to support his sick wife and small child. The movie was a commentary on Chaplin's disdain for capitalism and war. When released much of the public saw *Monsieur Verdoux* as further proof that Charlie Chaplin was a communist.

Charlie Chaplin in his first film, Making a Living.

Now the man who was born in England but had ingrained himself into American history and culture was no longer welcome in his adoptive home.

The child of two performers, Charlie Chaplin moved to America to pursue his own dreams of stardom. His first movie was in 1914 for Keystone Studios. One of Chaplin's most famous movies was also for Keystone Studios, the 1936 comedy *Modern Times*, which is not only important to Chaplin's career, but is also a reflection of his life prior to stardom and his political leanings. The toll from years of alcoholism claimed Chaplin's father when Chaplin was a young boy. His mother suffered from mental illness and was often admitted into psychiatric hospitals. His rough childhood drove him deeper into his art and shaped his personal beliefs. *Modern Times* shows Chaplin's timing and fast-paced wit as a writer, director, and actor. It also portrays

His rough childhood drove him

the conditions for factory workers as a series of dangerous tasks performed for their uncaring employers. Maybe the underlying message of *Modern Times* didn't catch on with the masses. Or maybe audiences related to the movie and wouldn't question Chaplin's patriotism until he became more vocal in the 1940s.

Knowing that if he were to return to the United States he would face intense questioning in court about his political leanings, he released a statement saying that McCarthyism "ha[s] created an unhealthy atmosphere in which liberal-minded individuals can be singled out and persecuted. Under these conditions I find it virtually impossible to continue my motion-picture work, and I have therefore given up my residence in the United States."

Chaplin made his new home in Sweden, where he made two more movies before retiring for good: *A King in New York* in 1957 and *A Countess from Hong Kong* in 1967. Chaplin had talked about making one more movie with his daughter, but it never came to fruition. In 1972 Chaplin briefly returned to the United States for one last time to receive an honorary Oscar for his lifetime achievement. He died in his sleep on Christmas day, 1977 from old age. Even in his later years when his health was failing, those who were close to Charlie Chaplin said he never lost his charm or goodwill.

deeper into his art
and shaped his personal beliefs.

Being Judy Garland is Quite a Chore

4

The Lost Autobiography

NO ONE CAN DENY THE ENORMOUS TALENT of Judy Garland. She had a voice many have tried to imitate and have failed. She was the American sweetheart who went over the rainbow. In 1963 she began narrating her life story into a reel-to-reel tape recorder. These tapes were to be transcribed and turned into her autobiography.

Judy Garland had a tumultuous life. Underneath the surface was a lifetime of emotional trauma. She could've started her autobiography with her childhood—the time her family was essentially run out of town after her father became the center of a homosexual scandal. It's been said he liked to sit in the back of the theater he owned and make sexual advances towards young men.

She could have started with her mother, who gave her pills to stay awake and peppy for auditions, then more pills to help her sleep at night. Or the MGM studio bosses who attempted to shame her into losing weight, gave her more pills (Benzedrine and Phenobarbital), and corseted her developing body into costumes to keep her looking childlike.

She could have complained about being the lowest paid actor in *The Wizard of Oz,* despite being the most talented. Or the time director Victor Fleming slapped her in the face for laughing too much during filming. Or the grueling work schedule she faced to make and promote the films she appeared in.

But what really seemed to be the target of her ire was Sid Luft (ex-husband number three), followed by the media, and then anything else that randomly crossed her mind.

These recordings cover a four-year span. Listening to all the tapes in one sitting plays like a one-woman show with frequent breaks to fill up on pharmaceuticals. Or the kind of drunken rambling one would expect to hear on their answering machine while their friend is going through a nasty divorce. The air around her must have been flammable.

The tapes begin with an impaired Judy Garland blowing into the microphone, testing it to make sure the recorder is on and slurring the words, "Now uh . . . Well . . . uh for openers, I don't know how to work this machine." She then refers to the reel-to-reel recorder as "an obvious Nazi machine" and "a Red China Manchurian candidate machine." She then does a quick change of gears and tears into the first round of Sid Luft bashing. "I wonder if Syd Luft's mother makes these machines . . . Could be she made all those machines . . . she made Syd . . . she spawned him in the . . . the uh . . . Red Seas."

Then she switches gears again: "I have the tenacity of a praying mantis. With a little black Irish witch involved." It's impressive that she could manage to use the word "tenacity" while her blood alcohol content bordered that of jet fuel.

The recordings go from rambling to downright bizarre after Judy returns from taking a break from the reel-to-reel. Maybe the pills and alcohol are really starting to kick in, or perhaps she ingested more during her breather. One thing is for certain, the next segment of what was to be her autobiography is every bit as confusing as Sarah Palin's interview with Katie Couric. "Uh . . . I can . . . always uh . . . truthfully say that nobody asked me.

When my number is up,

Nobody asked me. I was too little. When I went into vaudeville I was two years old and I just knew "Jingle Bells" and my grandmother threw me onto my father's stage. He owned a theater in Grand Rapids, Minnesota, and I just sang "Jingle Bells" and nobody told me to stop, so nobody ever asked me. Now I've never bothered to answer . . . because the questions have never been quite clear. But I can sit here now at a nifty age of forty-one and honestly say there's just me and this machine, *baby*." More smoker's cough, laughter. "I don't know whether anybody's interested or not but I am." Okay, so she *does* make more sense than the Palin/Couric interview.

This autobiographical stream of consciousness transforms into a piece of unintentional comedy that neither Andy Kaufman or Larry David could've belted out on their best days. Judy's rant about airplanes could have been right out of a Mel Brooks movie—had Mel just eaten a cereal bowl of pills and Jameson. "I've never met a cast of people I want to die with. You go on an airplane and look around at the people reading the *Reader's Digest* or whatever— you don't want to die with them. First place, you get . . . *I'd* get top billing: 'Judy Garland Dies in Plane Crash! For other . . . ughhh (long guttural noise) deceased turn to . . . section . . . B, page 18.' And then they state them alphabetically and they are a peculiar bunch." If the rest of the passengers are peculiar in comparison to Judy Garland, they're either straight as an arrow or *really* weird.

"What are we doing flying around in airplanes for one thing? We . . . we're not . . . not even birds go up that high."

"I have to make friends with the pilot and, uh, give his children my autograph whereupon he tells me that his children are

I want a new one

just as important to him as my life. Forget it! His life isn't nearly as important as my life is to me. Sheer selfishness, I don't really care about anybody but me." More smoker's cough, laughter. "And when my number is up, I want a new one and I have no intention of checking out. Now this machine isn't going to get me either. One way or another we're going to overcome it." Here she places a short, forced, scoffing laugh—the kind one would expect to hear when asking for ketchup at a fine steakhouse.

"I am funny!"

No segue; she goes right into her next rant.

"Inanimate objects just ruin me. I can check into a hotel to do a one-night stand concert . . . and try to go into the closet to get my dress off a hanger and an absolutely strange, strange mind you . . . little wire hanger without one thing on it flies off from left field and hits me in the nose . . . A lot of people have hit me in the nose . . . I've got a kinda nice nose."

The second part of her self-recorded autobiography ends with the declaration, "I, Judy Garland, am gonna talk and everybody better just sit on the bench and watch the ballgame." The click of the machine is audible—as if the stop button had been pushed in triumph.

When Garland returns for round three, she somehow manages to sound even more intoxicated, almost like she's falling asleep. The listener can imagine the reel-to-reel tape recorder is the only thing keeping her head from bashing into the table.

"I'm outraged." She begins while sounding anything but. Her words clumsily pour into each other while she verbally doc-

"Being Judy Garland is

uments her mistreatment by the press. "I can't rise above it, the scandalous obscene lies that have been . . . the so-called printed word . . . and I can't rise above the gossip mongers. Well, all of it has affected my children, my health, and my work."

"I've spent . . . years and years and years trying to please through singing or acting . . . there's nothing wrong with that and yet I've constantly been written . . . or talked about . . . by certain individuals that I'll get to later . . . as an unfit person. Well what kind of people are they?! They're dead people. But they've tried to kill me along the way and by God they won't. They won't! Because I'm mad!"

The machine stops again, and when Garland returns she's in better spirits. She speaks with genuine gratitude for the companionship of her then fiancé, Mark Herron, who became husband number four out of five. In the midst of coughs and deep swallowing, she talks of her appreciation of Herron, who loved her even when she wasn't singing and dancing, "I'm very proud. It's made me prettier than ever."

For a moment, the one-sided conversation becomes more human, and a very real and deep love, admiration, and pride for her daughter Liza emerges. "But we have a love. My little boy, Joe. My little girl, Lorna. My young lady . . . grown-up daughter, Liza. Mark, myself, we have a love that makes everything else look just *stupid*." The way she spits out the word "stupid" throws the audio Tilt-A-Whirl back into another dip, bringing her back to husband number three: "Sid Luft . . . is an animal. He's just some kind of breed. And I'll tell the world whenever I can that he's a thief . . . a blackmailer, a sadist . . . and a man who doesn't even care one bit one way or the other about any

quite a chore."

other living soul, let alone his nice children. He's told them how untalented they are, how stupid they are, who needs them, he's told them how he doesn't like them. That's a nice man, that's a big upstanding *tramp*!"

Sid Luft, the amateur boxer once known as "One-Punch Luft," was the producer of the remake *A Star Is Born* starring Garland. During the production Garland claimed illness, causing budget overruns. After production, an additional thirty minutes of film was cut to allow more screenings per day at theaters. The problems during filming and postproduction caused the film to

Sid Luft . . . is an animal. He's just some kind of breed.

lose money. Because of this loss, Garland did not obtain profits she had been expecting. Garland nor Luft made any more movies for Warner after the fiasco.

Eventually the marriage to Sid Luft dissolved under the stress of financial and emotional problems. Luft filed for custody of the children while Judy Garland became engaged and moved to London. Her frustrations over these custody issues are mentioned on the tape: "Well maybe he's in with the . . . judges (the word "judges" is slurred so badly it has three syllables) . . . in Santa Monica court so that I can't even get to see my children now that I live in England. Being Judy Garland is quite a chore."

In the midst of all the rambling, Judy Garland says something that gives the listener an honest look into her emotions. This time it's not the ranting, angry side of Judy Garland but

"Don't make a joke of

what the ranting and anger are trying to cover up: "Sure I've been loved. By the public . . . I can't take the public home with me." And in a split second she's angry and shouting again.

Sid Luft goes right back into the line of fire and is accused of being "paranoick." "Let him get his fanny out and go to work!" she barks. "I'm not paying for him anymore." "I hate that word (man) in connection with Sid Luft. Michael Sidney Luft is not a man, he's not a father, he's not a worker, he's not a contributor, he's not anything! He's a pimp."

The next act is ready. The machine clicks back into action, the tape hissing as it runs across the magnetic heads. The voice of Judy Garland sounds more together and yet much more desperate. She pleads for readers to hear her side of things, wanting to set the record straight. "Believe me, the way you believed me when I sang all those songs!" She pleads to be seen as human and not just a wind-up entertainer. Her voice is heavy and sorrowful: "Don't make a joke of me anymore." She gives herself a moment to reflect on specific barbs that bore her name. For the first time in these recordings she flat out denies having a drug or alcohol addiction. She shouts that it's a "God damned wonder" that she doesn't. From shouts to whispers, she recites the names of her children and fiancé as the reasons she doesn't.

Having acknowledged the scandal of her addictions, she finally acknowledges her own speech: "When I play back the tapes I hear that I slur my words very badly, but that doesn't make too much difference as long as my thoughts are not slurred."

Again she breaks into song with a lounge performance of, "How Do You Feel?" A piano plays while her words bungle out. A performance reserved for last call at an off strip bar. This is

me anymore."

not a shining moment. It's a memorable performance for all the wrong reasons. Think of William Shatner's melancholy performance of "Rocket Man." Garland's rendition is every bit as bad but without any of the camp.

As the one-woman rollercoaster turns the final bend, the machine clicks back on to Judy Garland singing, "Since I Lost My Man." It's the voice of a drunk who starts to sober up as the sun rises. The song itself is one of lament and loss. Garland's singing makes the song more desperate; what should sound strong and soulful comes out as anger.

The autobiography never materialized. Judy Garland married for a fifth and final time to Mickey Deans on March 15, 1969. On June 22, 1969, Deans found Garland's body in their bathroom—cause of death was an accidental drug overdose. She was forty-seven years old.

Things you may not have known about America's most over-hyped Awards Show

5

Oscar Oddities

ఈు ఎఏ

RECOGNITION IS A GOOD THING. THERE'S absolutely nothing wrong in acknowledging a job well done in any field. However, the Academy Awards have become so overblown (and perceived by some to be totally driven by politics and ass kissing) that, to some, the golden statuettes have ceased to be symbols of achievement and have become all but meaningless. Over the years some real Oscar Oddities have taken place—enough to fill an entire book. Below is a timeline of some interesting tidbits and misfires that happened on Hollywood's "prom night."

1927 The Academy Awards are born! Originally called the International Academy of Motion Picture Arts and Sciences, then later shortened by dropping the word "International," the awards ceremony needed a trophy to give away to the winners. Art director Cedric Gibbons was given the task to design the trophy. While attending a meeting to plan the first Academy Awards ceremony, Gibbons heard planners talk about how a strong image was needed and how the five branches of the film industry (actors, writers, directors, technicians, and producers) needed to be represented. While still at the meeting, Gibbons made a sketch of a naked man plunging a sword into a five-holed reel of film. A run of statuettes was commissioned, and the use of Gibbons' original concept continues to this day. (Why the man had to be naked, and why he was holding a sword . . . no one seems to know.)

1948 The movie industry was taking two major hits. First, television was finding its way into American homes, which resulted in fewer ticket sales at the theater. Second, the Supreme Court notified the studios that owning both theater chains and the studios was in violation of antitrust laws. The ruling meant the major studios, who helped fund the Academy Awards ceremony, were about to lose roughly half of their income. Spending needed to be scaled back, and one of the first expenses to go was funding to the Academy Awards. Because of the loss of funds, the ceremony was held in a theater with 950 seats, a stark comparison to the auditorium that had been used in the past with 6,700 seats. Voting members of the Academy began to complain that they saw no reason to fork out their yearly dues (thirty-six dollars at the time) if they weren't able to attend the ceremony. *The Hollywood Reporter* ran an article stating that the film industry was "playing poverty" and needed to show signs to the movie-going public that they were still kicking. So the studios began planning post-ceremony parties. Right— no money to go towards the actual event celebrating the movies they made, but money was available for the lavish and self-congratulatory parties that followed. Good work.

1950 Actress Judy Holliday was under investigation for having Communist leanings. Her name was listed in *Red Channels: The Report of Communist Influence in Radio and Television*, which contained the names of 151 movie-industry types suspected to be Communist sympathizers. When Holliday's *Born Yesterday* was released in 1950, a Catholic newspaper, *Tidings*, said the

"Jane Wyman, who's been putting off that kidney operation,

(left) Judy Holliday was listed in Red Channels, a publication that named suspected Communists in the film industry. (right) Despite the efforts of writer Mike Connolly, Jane Wyman did not get the sympathy vote from the Academy in 1951. Vivien Leigh stole the show with her portrayal of Blanche DuBois in A Streetcar Named Desire and took the Best Actress award.

movie was "communistic," which resulted in picketing at theaters screening the film. However, J. Edgar Hoover announced that no connection could be found between Judy Holliday and the Communist Party. Later Holliday would win the Academy Award for Best Actress. But she did not accept the award in person. Perhaps she was in a meeting that was running late. . . .

1951 In an attempt to help his friend bring home the big award, writer Mike Connolly began drumming up false concern about the health of actress Jane Wyman, who had starred in *The Blue Veil*, a drama about a widow who becomes a nurse who takes care of young children. In hopes of gaining sympathy votes, Connolly had written, "Jane Wyman, who's been putting off that kidney operation, may find herself in the hospital along about Oscar time." Gee, I wonder what he's getting at? Connolly's thinly veiled attempts didn't work. Jane Wyman lost the Best Actress award to Vivien Leigh for her portrayal of Blanche DuBois in *A Streetcar Named Desire*.

may find herself in the hospital along about Oscar time."

Mike Connolly did not extend the favor in **1952** when he wrote of fellow writer Michael Wilson, who previously won an Academy Award for *A Place in the Sun*. Connolly said to Academy voters, "If you give unfriendly witness Michael Wilson another Oscar this year, you'll be giving the Academy a body blow from which it may never recover." Michael Wilson had plead the fifth during the McCarthy Communist witch hunt, which caused him to be labeled a Communist and blacklisted. If only Michael Wilson needed a kidney operation . . .

1963 Roddy McDowall was thought to be a shoo-in for Best Supporting Actor for his role as Octavian Caesar Augustus, the evil cousin of Cleopatra, played by Elizabeth Taylor, in *Cleopatra*. But McDowall would not receive so much as a nomination due to an error made by Twentieth Century Fox Studios. McDowall could not be nominated for Best Supporting Actor because Fox had listed the entire cast as "Leading Players." Twentieth Century Fox Studios attempted to fight the technicality, but the Academy would only agree to change the rule for following years to allow the Academy to determine what category a performer would best fit. The Academy also purchased ad space in trade papers to clear up any confusion, stating that, while critics agree McDowall's performance was award worthy, it would not be eligible, ". . . due to a regrettable error on the part of Twentieth Century Fox."

1963 In *Lilies of the Field*, Sidney Poitier played a construction worker who travels from job to job, living in his car. He is hired by a group of nuns who have fled Berlin and are now attempting to establish a community in the United States. Poitier and the head nun argue about who is building their place of worship: Is it Poitier or God, who is simply using Poitier as a tool? Though the premise may sound lackluster, Poitier proved his weight as an actor and was awarded with a nomination for Best Actor in a Leading Role. Poitier was cautious in his optimism. The *New York Times* had referred to the movie as *"Going My Way* with a Negro." Poitier was quoted as saying, "What if eight million Negroes decide to kick in their TV screens at the moment someone else's name is called?" No one would find out, because Poitier won the award. After the ceremony he told reporters, "I'd like to think it will help someone, but I don't believe my Oscar will be a sort of magic wand that will wipe away the restrictions on job opportunities for Negro actors."

"What if eight million Negroes decide to kick in their TV screens . . ."

1967 Twentieth Century Fox attempted to catch the magic Disney found in *Mary Poppins* with *Doctor Dolittle*. Archer Winsten, film critic of the *New York Post*, wrote of *Doctor Dolittle,* "I'm not going to pretend I wasn't bored silly." The critics were harsh and so were the audiences. *Doctor Dolittle* managed to recoup only one third of its production costs. This didn't stop Twentieth Century Fox from trying to bring home the gold. A memo from a studio publicist began to circulate, stating, "The following has been decided regarding our Academy Award campaign for *Doctor Dolittle*. Each screening will be preceded by champagne or cocktails and a buffet dinner in the studio commissary. *Doctor Dolittle* is the studio's prime target for Academy Award consideration." The studio gimmick was well received, making the other studios a little nervous. Fox's ploy resulted in a mixed bag on Oscar night. *Doctor Dolittle* received nine nominations but only won two trophies—for Best Song and Best Vi-

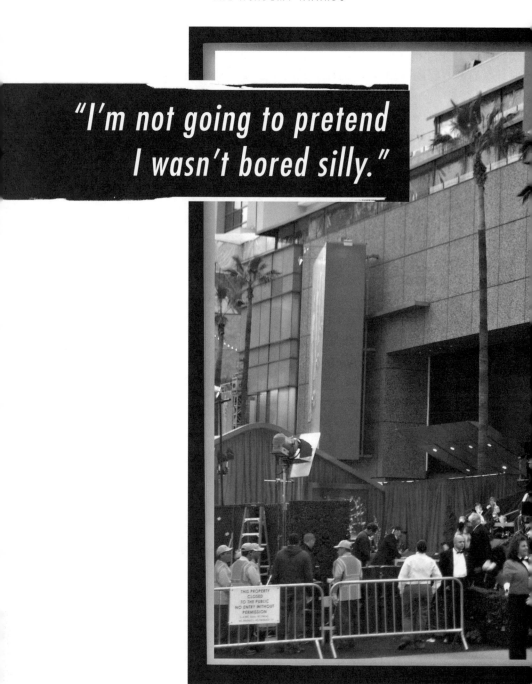

"I'm not going to pretend I wasn't bored silly."

"The (Academy Awards) ceremonies are a two-hour meat parade."

sual Effects. So, was the studio able to "buy" awards for a movie that flopped at the box office and was panned by critics? What do you think?

1970 George C. Scott was nominated for his portrayal of World War II commander, General George S. Patton. The real Patton was a strict leader who accepted no excuses for weakness and was often criticized for bluntly vocalizing his opinions. George C. Scott studied for the role extensively, and his hard work paid off. Many consider Patton to be George C. Scott's finest work—and he won the Academy Award. But Scott felt that acting was an art, not a competition, and he returned the award, stating he was not in competition with other actors. He was later quoted as saying, "The (Academy Awards) ceremonies are a two-hour meat parade, a public display with contrived suspense for economic reasons."

"Any Jewish person who goes to see that

1977 Vanessa Redgrave was getting lots of attention—both wanted *and* unwanted. She was receiving rave reviews for her title role in the movie *Julia*. She was also drawing fire from the JDL (Jewish Defense League) for her political work, attempting to establish a homeland for the Palestinian people, hanging out with PLO (Palestinian Liberation Organization) leader Yasir Arafat, and producing a political propaganda film called *The Palestinians*. When Fox Studios failed to issue a statement denouncing Redgrave's political actions, the JDL began picketing theaters showing *Julia*. Reports surfaced of JDL members also letting live mice loose in theaters. When these actions failed to produce the desired results, a letter was issued to the Academy, warning of the protests that would follow should Vanessa Redgrave be nominated. In part the letter read, "She transcends art by her politics. Any Jewish person who goes to see that picture ought to have their head examined. You might just as well see Hitler's girlfriend and encourage her."

Redgrave was nominated and won for Best Supporting Actress. During her acceptance speech she told the audience, "I think you should be very proud that in the last few weeks you have stood firm, and you have refused to be intimidated by the threats of a small bunch of Zionist hoodlums whose behavior is an insult to the stature of Jews all over the world and to their great and heroic record of struggle against fascism and oppression. And I pledge to you that I will continue to fight against anti-Semitism and fascism."

Redgrave has claimed to be on a neo-Nazi hit list. So neither the JDL nor the Nazis wanted her. The real question now is, where is the political organization to find Vanessa Redgrave a homeland of her own?

picture ought to have their head examined."

1985 Steven Spielberg had already made a place for himself in cinematic history by creating the films *E.T.*, *Close Encounters of the Third Kind*, and *Raiders of the Lost Ark*. It wasn't until Spielberg was given the book *The Color Purple* to read during a flight that he had the desire to make a serious drama. When all was said and done, *The Color Purple* received eleven nominations from the Academy Award panel. The movie was nominated for everything from Best Picture to Best Costume Design, but there was one name, one nomination, missing from the list, and it stuck out like a missing index finger. Steven Spielberg was not nominated for Best Director. Spielberg did not publicly comment, but the studio released a written statement that many felt the director had a hand in penning. The letter was published in the trade papers under purchased ad space. The letter expressed appreciation, however, "At the same time, the company is shocked and dismayed that the movie's primary creative force, Steven Spielberg, was not recognized."

The published letter spurred reporter Martin Grove to suggest, ". . . that the balloting not take place under a cloud." He also suggested an investigation to see if there had been "any organized effort to dissuade voters from nominating Spielberg." Academy member Henry Jaglom responded to Grove in an interview to the *Los Angeles Times,* telling them, "He (Spielberg) took this wonderful material and turned it into zip-a-dee-doo-dah *Song of the South.*"

It is not known for certain if the words in the letter came from Spielberg himself or if the backhanded compliment had any impact on the judges' voting, but *The Color Purple* won none of the eleven categories it had been nominated in. Not even Whoopi Goldberg, who deserved it more for her role as Celie Johnson than she did as a wisecracking medium in *Ghost*.

1990 Martin Scorsese made what is one of the best, if not *the* best, movie ever made—*Goodfellas*. Scorsese's directing and Michael Ballhaus' cinematography were perfect. To this day, the one-take shot of Henry and Karen entering the club is used as an example of flow, where cast and crew work with impeccably timed precision. Writer Nicholas Pileggi has provided America with one of the best anti-heroes ever known—Henry Hill—a man who rises from nothing to have it all. The problem is everything he has is provided by a life of crime. Even though Henry Hill is an unpleasant person you'd never want your kids around, you can't help but like him. And you can't help but like him largely because Ray Liotta is so solid in the role. *Goodfellas* is the ultimate "rise and fall story," a Greek tragedy with guns. So when the Oscars came around, Scorsese was crushed under a mountain of gold statues, right? Wrong. *Goodfellas* received

one, *one*, Academy Award, which went to Joe Pesci for his portrayal of short-fused gangster Tony DeVito.

    Goodfellas lost out to *Dances With Wolves* for Best Picture.
Lorraine Bracco lost out to Whoopi Goldberg for Best Support-
ing Actress for *Ghost*. Kevin Costner beat Martin Scorsese for
Best Director with *Dances With Wolves*, which also beat out
Goodfellas for best screenplay based on material from another
medium. Finally, *Dances With Wolves* beat *Goodfellas* for best
editing. Watch *Dances With Wolves* and then watch *Goodfellas*.
Which is the better movie? Watch anything Whoopi Goldberg
has done and compare it to anything Lorraine Bracco has done.
Anything. Who is the better actress? The Academy Awards isn't
a popularity contest, right? Right.

Martin Scorsese

PAUL BERN

The
Darkest
Comedy

6

A Shocking and Puzzling Death

တာ

PAUL BERN WAS DEAD. THE GERMAN immigrant who made a living writing, producing, and directing in Hollywood was found dead in his home on September 5, 1932. He was forty-two years old.

Bern had worked with Greta Garbo and John Barrymore. He was married to the beautiful young actress Jean Harlow, who would also be dead almost five years later. The death of Paul Bern was shocking. The evidence left behind was puzzling. Bern was found naked with a single gunshot wound to the head. Near his body was a note that read—

> Dearest Dear, Unfortuately [sic] this is the only way to make good the frightful wrong I have done you and to wipe out my abject humiliation, I Love [sic] you.
> Paul
> You understand that last night was only a comedy

Last night was only a comedy? What happened last night? The police definitely wanted to know. The public was dying to know. The most embarrassing rumors began to circulate, but poor, dead Paul Bern was unable to defend himself. Bern was said to be impotent, incapable of satisfying his twenty-one-year-old bride in bed. Paul Bern was called a pervert and the "comedy" that he had referred to was a deep-seated obsession with some fetish. Possibly the most embarrassing gossip was that his genitals were so underdeveloped he was incapable of performing.

The death wasn't reported until the next morning. Words like "mysterious," "puzzling," and "mystifying" peppered the headlines along with the word "suicide." The papers talked about the letter Paul left, and soon the press was searching for Jean Harlow, who had left the night of Paul's death to have dinner with her parents. Her parents told reporters Jean was devastated, sedated, and unable to comment.

Trying to keep the powder keg of gossip under control, MGM studio bosses told their employees that Bern should never have married Jean Harlow and that Bern knew he was impotent and shot himself out of shame. Some spoke up: There was no way Bern was impotent. Producer and cofounder of MGM, Louis B. Mayer, said a doctor would testify that he was, if further proof was needed. It was understood, if asked, shame and impotence drove Paul Bern to shoot himself. Sympathy for Jean Harlow would be immense. That sympathy, the studio hoped, would also raise her star status.

Paul Bern was buried September 9, 1932. Jean Harlow cried quietly throughout the services. But where was the grief-stricken Jean when Paul was killed? Some say she was simply at her parent's house for dinner when the death occurred. Another story wove a much more tangled web. Twenty years earlier Paul Bern had been involved with Dorothy Millette, a struggling young actress whom Paul had met in an acting class. One morning Bern found Millette in an unexplainable comatose state from which, doctors said, she would never recover. Bern placed Millette in a hospital and made sure she received the care she needed. But it appeared to be true that she would never recover: Dorothy

Bern was found naked with a

Millette was not getting better; she remained unresponsive. And while Paul Bern did still care for her, his heart eventually moved on.

Years later, he became infatuated with a struggling actress, Jean Harlow. She was young, good looking, and talented enough to convince Bern she needed to be a star. He fought for the actress, convincing MGM to at least give her a screen test—which Paul Bern paid for out of his own pocket. He pushed to get Jean the starring role in *Red Headed Woman* (1931), and eventually she got it.

When production was complete, a preview screening was shown to test audiences, receiving overwhelmingly positive feedback. After the screening, Bern and Harlow kissed in the back of their chauffeured car. They married soon after the official release of *Red Headed Woman* in 1932. Paul never told Jean about Dorothy Millette, and, just as if their real life had entered the pages of one of their scripts, Dorothy awoke from her coma.

Not only had Dorothy Millette awakened, she had no idea Paul had moved on and married another woman. When she discovered Bern had moved out West, she boarded a train from New York to San Francisco. From there she checked into the Plaza Hotel and contacted Bern with the hope of picking up their romance again. Bern had told a friend he decided to make things right. He would tell Millette it was over and then eventually tell Jean of his past. A date was made for Millette to visit Bern at his home. Stories vary, but Bern then either sent his wife off to have dinner with her parents or purposefully provoked a fight so she would spend the night with her parents.

In any case, Harlow left for the evening. A neighbor said

single gunshot wound to the head.

they saw a veiled woman leave the property in a car during the night but could not give a better description. Dorothy Millette checked out of the Plaza Hotel and left no forwarding information. Her body was found soon after floating in the Sacramento River near Walnut Grove. She had jumped to her death from a boat, the *Delta King*. No one claimed her body.

Jean Harlow was a young widow, Dorothy Millette was a suicide, and Paul Bern was a big question mark.

Friederike Marcus, Paul Bern's sister, released a statement to the press on the day of his funeral: "The dearest soul on earth is laid to rest today. Life had everything for him to enjoy to the utmost capacity. He loved his work and his surroundings. He had faced many big problems in his life, many big heartaches, but he always faced the music." The statement continued to what would really catch the public's attention, "About twenty years ago he fell in love with a girl by the name of Dorothy Millette. He was never married to her, but he lived with her for several years. Then she became sick and was admitted into a sanatorium.

"Paul was heartbroken; the man went around like a shadow. He mourned like he mourned for a dead one. He did not take his life." The point was clear: Paul Bern was not the type one expected to kill himself. Friederike later says in the same statement, "Then along came Jean. He thought he was the luckiest man on earth to find all that he wanted. It was a short dream because two months later he took his own life."

Bern was said to be impotent.

Her statement resumed, "He was more to me than a brother. He told me many of his secrets, and told me many times how he spent his life in the company of young girls, living with many of them in Hollywood, and enjoying life to the greatest extent."

Friederike ended her with, ". . . if he found life unbearable now, then let him rest and sleep as he deserves to sleep. A big soul, a big heart, and a big character have been laid to rest."

Jean Harlow

PETER JACKSON'S

BAD TASTE

PETER JACKSON

Shock

and

Awful!

7

Peter Jackson Eats Vomit, Wins Oscar

BEFORE PETER JACKSON CAME ALONG, NEW Zealanders were best known for becoming irate when being mistaken for Australians. This would change when Peter Jackson, who was born in 1961 on Halloween in the small coastal village of Pukerua Bay, became a movie-making dynamo. As a child, Peter saw the 1933 classic monster movie *King Kong* on television. The stop animation caught his imagination. The story of the giant, misunderstood ape with a pure heart won him over. It was a defining moment: Peter Jackson decided he was going to be a filmmaker. In an interview, Jackson told reporter Stone Phillips, "I got my parents' little Super 8 camera, and I tried to animate this rubber Kong that I made, and I had a cardboard model of the Empire State Building. I was this sort of ambitious twelve-year-old. I spent more time making the models than I did actually filming."

At seventeen Jackson dropped out of school. He got a job as a photo engraver at the *Evening Post*. Never taking his eye off the prize, Jackson was putting together resources to make his first movie. His first venture would be *Bad Taste*, a movie where aliens harvest humans for an intergalactic fast food chain. The low budget did not stop Jackson from squeezing tons of vile gags into the movie—including a scene where Jackson, playing one of the aliens, eats a bowl of vomit.

Jackson made all the props in *Bad Taste* himself. Guns were carved out of wood. Latex pieces were molded in his mother's home and baked in her oven. The notorious vomit eaten by the alien villains was a mixture of yogurt, muesli, and green food coloring. When filming was complete, Jackson took his movie to National Film Unit, a production company in New Zealand. NFU was known as a one-stop postproduction studio. From beginning to end, it took more than four years to complete his first movie.

Bad Taste was released in 1987, becoming a hit with fans of horror and drive-in style movies. The censorship board of Queensland, Australia, banned the film due to its numerous scenes of violence and depravity. Though his brand of humor and love for gore gags were shocking, Jackson proved he knew how to make a movie on a tiny budget.

In 1989 Jackson's next project emerged—a perverted reimaging of what it would be like behind the scenes of *The Muppet Show* if the Muppets were junkies, murderers, and drug addicts . . . like the rest of Hollywood. *Meet the Feebles* is acted out entirely with puppets engaging in the most perverse and obscene activities that even Paris Hilton and Brad Renfro couldn't dream up. *Meet the Feebles* received a limited release, and critics proclaimed Jackson's work to be deplorable and admirable at the same time. James Berardinelli of ReelViews.net called the movie, "disgustingly graphic, obscenely offbeat, and caustically funny"

Peter Jackson brought forth one of the most celebrated comedy horror movies made to date. Appearing in 1992, *Braindead* (or *Dead Alive* as it's known in the U.S.) plays out like a Three Stooges skit invaded by zombies. The lead character, Lionel, is a hapless but likeable guy trying to keep his undead mother away from the public. A store clerk named Paquita is convinced Lionel is her soul mate after a Tarot reading. The two continue to cross paths and their love develops. The movie has a five-minute scene of Lionel cutting up zombies with a lawn mower, and Paquita

Jackson's penchant for splatter, blood and vomit

sharing a kiss with Lionel while he is covered in entrails and gore.

Jackson's penchant for splatter, blood and vomit had many New Zealanders apprehensive about how the real-life murder of his next project would be portrayed. As it turned out, *Heavenly Creatures* would be the proving ground that Peter Jackson was more than a horror director with a keen wit. The story is of two New Zealand girls who used their love for fantasy to escape the real world, where they are awkward and unpopular. The mother of one of the girls begins to worry that their friendship might be leading into a lesbian relationship and forbids them to see each other. Seeing no other option, the two girls savagely beat the mother to death.

If Jackson wanted to, he could have taken the lowbrow road, making light of the movie's events with over-the-top blood sprays. But he showed real finesse in depicting the two girls, as each gradually becomes the only person the other can relate to. So when their relationship becomes forbidden, it is believable for them to feel they have no other option. The movie is a genuine look into mental illness and social disconnection.

Jackson and co-writer Fran Walsh (whom Jackson had met during postproduction for *Bad Taste*) were nominated for Best Screenplay in the mother of all awards ceremonies, the Academy Awards. He was legitimized as an artist by the most powerful film industry in the world. He didn't win, but his fans were amazed the man was even getting recognition!

Now Hollywood was paying attention to what the large, bearded kiwi intended to work on next. He achieved minimal mainstream success on his next comedy horror film *The Frighteners* in 1996. The movie followed a widower played by Michael J.

had many New Zealanders
apprehensive

Fox, who used his ability to see and communicate with ghosts to scam the living. The grift ends up going awry. Fox needs to solve a supernatural serial killer mystery before he, or the first woman he's cared about since his wife's death, becomes the next victim.

The Frighteners was rated R. There are scenes of violence and people being terrorized, but the movie lacked the over-the-top gore gags Jackson fans wanted. Compared to exploits filmed in *Braindead*, *The Frighteners* feels like a strong PG-13. The movie did win an award for special effects at the Catalonian International Film Festival. But mainly *The Frighteners* was overlooked, and only established Peter Jackson fans loved it.

In 1998 Peter Jackson bought the National Film Unit (NFU) where he had completed work on *Bad Taste*. He is a strong believer in working locally and supporting local workers as much as possible. He said with fondness of the company, "If (the Film Unit) had closed, I would have had to go on a plane to Sydney a lot, which would have been pretty boring." The business has since been renamed to Park Road Post.

One can only imagine how hard it was to film all three Lord of the Rings movies at the same time. Jackson referred to it as "laying the tracks down in front of the train as it was moving forward." Many felt translating the Tolkien books to film was impossible. Considering that everything about Jackson's career seemed impossible, it was the perfect project for him. All three books would be filmed at once for a total cost of $180 million dollars. It took over three years to complete the three movies, 274 days of shooting, and up to seven different units filming at the same time—which resulted in hours upon hours of raw footage to sort through.

Lord of the Rings: The Fellowship of the Ring was released in the United States on December 19, 2001. Unanimously the supporters and naysayers declared, "Jackson has done it!" The movie is a sweeping fantasy shot in New Zealand but will have you believing in another world where hobbits and orcs live. From the special effects, to the acting, to the storytelling, *The Fellowship of the Ring* was captivating. Audiences could barely wait another year to see the next installment.

The Academy took notice of the major accomplishment, lavishing the first installment with thirteen nominations. On the night of the awards ceremony, there sat Peter Jackson among Hollywood's elite, hair unkempt. Hell, now *he* was part of Hollywood's elite, but it didn't change who Peter Jackson was. He looked like someone dressed a homeless man in a tux and gave him a seat.

The other two installments, *The Two Towers* and *The Return of the King*, were released to much fanfare and critical praise. When Oscar time rolled around, *The Return of the King* received eleven nominations. Come Oscar night *The Return of the King* won all eleven categories it was nominated for. Peter Jackson was the first person since James L. Brooks made *Terms of Endearment* (1983) to win Best Director, Best Writing/Adapted Screenplay, and Best Picture. In sixteen years Peter Jackson had gone from eating vomit to winning case after case of awards. If there has ever been a man for his time and place, it's Peter Jackson.

But what about all his old fans—the ones who were there in the beginning watching Jackson create movies where zombie babies can tear clean through a woman's head? In a 2005 interview with Cinecon, Jackson was asked if the man who made *Braindead* and *Bad Taste* still existed after all the commercial success. Jackson replied, "Oh absolutely. I hope to one day get to make another low-budget horror film." Should the now slim-and-trim Jackson return to his roots, he will find his fan base is still there.

Peter Jackson with Jack Black during the filming of King Kong. As a kid, Jackson was a fan of the 1933 version of King Kong. In fact, it was the film that first inspired him to be a filmmaker.

RICHARD ELFMAN

The **Last** and **Greatest** Midnight Movie

Ever Made

8

The Forbidden Zone

ഇരൻ

THE YEAR WAS 1982 WHEN THE LIGHTS dimmed and a projector sputtered the first frames of what many considered the last and greatest midnight movie ever made. Getting the future classic made wasn't easy. Getting it shown in theaters proved to be even harder. But a cult following and home video gave *Forbidden Zone* its place in movie history.

Like Lewis Carroll with much cheaper

Louisville film critic Alan Abbott summed up *Forbidden Zone* best when he called it, "A deeply weird film, overflowing with intentional non sequiturs and continuity errors. Like Lewis Carroll with much cheaper and more problematic drugs." The story does follow an *Alice in Wonderland* kind of tale where characters leave reality and enter the "sixth dimension." A land where women run wild wearing nothing but panties; where Hervé Villechaize is king; where Susan Tyrell, a woman who dwarfed normal-sized men in every aspect of the word, is queen. In the sixth dimension, frogs are butlers, punishment is sometimes the reward, and everywhere is music.

It all began with a man named Richard Elfman, who had been performing with a theater troupe called The Mystic Knights of Oingo Boingo. The group had traveled extensively, at times carrying two large truck trailers full of props, set pieces, and musical equipment. They even appeared on *The Gong Show,* where they won the top prize. (The footage can be found on the Internet.) Richard can be seen dancing around the stage in a giant rocket costume.

Some time after *The Gong Show,* Richard decided to walk away from his theater troup, leaving his younger brother, Danny, at the helm. He began writing a script with fellow Mystic Knights cohort, Matthew Bright. It was the first time either of them attempted to take on a project this big. Elfman used his real-life neighbors, whom he described as trashy, for the "general idea" to form the movie's main characters. Their real-life antics did not

and more problematic drugs.

make it to the screen, but their personas did. And so the Hercules family was created. A family so vile they swear, name call, expel gas, and fight at the breakfast table. Yet, the Elfman spin makes them odd and fascinating.

Frenchy, the daughter of the Hercules family, discovers that the doorway to the sixth deminsion is in their basement. Once she enters, her friends and family soon follow—some in search of Frenchy (as well as her transvestite classmate who has also disappeared) and others by total accident (like her father, who rockets into the sixth dimension as a result of a workplace explosion at a tar pit factory).

The humor remains steady throughout the movie but at times the jokes go from absurd to dark. Elfman attributes the darker aspects of the film to Matthew Bright's sense of humor. He says, "The scene where Squeezit (played by Matthew Bright, who is supposed to be a child) meets his father was originally written with the sailor (Squeezit's father) beating the shit out of Chicken Boy (aka Squeezit) . . . really wiping the walls and floor with him. I had to cut it for practical/logistical reasons."

A family so **vile** they swear, name call,

After much writing and rewriting, Elfman and Bright completed their script and were ready to move forward. Sets were being built and actors were being cast. Some of the characters would be played by Mystic Knight members. Other roles would need to be filled with hired actors. Then there was the weirdness of several scenes that call for a train of young women running past the camera wearing nothing but panties. How did a man funding a movie out of his own pocket fill all these roles? Elfman says, "My old pal and Mystic Knight cofounder Gene Cunningham (listed in the movies credits as Ugh Fudge-bwana) also put in money. So did Carl Borack, who ultimately saved the production when I went broke. In terms of actors, Matthew helped find Susan Tyrrell, Hervé Villechaize, and Joe Spinell, who played Squeezit's dad." At the time Villechaize and Matthew Bright were roommates.

With everything in place, Richard Elfman stepped into his many roles on the production. How many titles did he have? "Just director, producer, actor, voice over, janitor," he says. Although he had lots of stage experience, he had never directed before. "On one of the first days on set, an older crew guy asked what qualified me to direct this project. Someone else chimed in, 'He's paying us!'" And with that quip, unexposed film spun behind the camera lens into infamy.

What the ensemble produced was lo-fi art at its best. Handmade set pieces were inspired by "German Expressionism, *The Cabinet of Dr. Caligari*, with some Max Fleischer thrown in for good measure," says Elfman. The original release was shot in black and white, with the stark backdrops standing out like set pieces in a live-action Betty Boop cartoon. The musical numbers kick in like you're in a club filled with jazz musicians on LSD . . .

expel gas, and fight at the breakfast table.

all the madness spins around your head.

A bizarre script, amateur actors, handmade sets . . . the whole production was a nonstop train of weirdness. How did the cast work together while the movie was being shot?

Hervé Villechaize and Susan Tyrrell had been dating before production. They were no longer an item, but that didn't stop the occasional outburst. Elfman said of the two, "A few times they had emotional fights on the set. Also surreal. She had a booming voice, a product of years of stage work with New York's Lincoln Center Repertory Company. Hervé had a small voice box. From the distance, all you could hear was her." Perhaps some of that tension carried over while filming. Elfman describes a scene where Villechaize and Tyrrel's characters, the king and queen of the sixth dimension, argue: "When Susan and Hervé did the King and Queen jealousy fight around the table, Susan hit him really hard in the kidneys with an orange. His inner organs were overly squeezed, and it really hurt the guy."

Elfman shot back at the negative reputation Hervé Villechaize has carried. "I was impressed by his charisma. Tiny stature, *huge* presence. A bit surreal, the dichotomy of those two factors. But he had a great sense of humor, and we became good friends." Villechaize also showed how he believed in both art and the project, "He stuck with the project even though we had production shutdowns for months at a time. He came on weekends and painted sets. *He kicked his check back in the production.* The guy was always professional, and he added great humor and charm to the set. Although he did own guns, and liked to show them off." Villechaize was already working in television at this time, so he could have commanded a high salary. Elfman says, "His agent at the time tried to get Hervé a huge fee. Hervé said he didn't want the money. Then the agent did everything under the sun to prevent Hervé from doing *Forbidden Zone*—even tried to convince me that doing *Forbidden Zone* while shooting *Fantasy Island* would kill Hervé. (This line only came up after the agent realized we had no money—before that he was happy to "kill" Hervé, as long the agent got his 10 percent.)"

Susan Tyrrell was previously nominated for an Oscar (Best Supporting Actress) in 1972's *Fat City*. Because Tyrrell had received a nod from the industry's top honor, you might think that she would be . . . difficult to deal with. When reflecting on working with Tyrrell, Elfman recalls, "My God! What a unique and talented woman! For whatever reasons, her life was not destined for the success she could have had. After receiving an Academy Award nomination for her *first* screen role, she ran away to Morocco for a year rather than schmooze with agents in Hollywood (as the success book might dictate). Susan was very enthusiastic on the set, a great trouper. Long hours, grueling nights, she refused a paycheck. I'm still in awe of Susan Tyrrell."

Susan Tyrrell wasn't the only talent on set with an Oscar connection. Joe Spinell, who plays a sailor meeting his son, Squeezit, for the first time, had a small role in 1972's *The Godfather*. It's not the same as having Brando, but it's fascinating to see the worlds of art cinema and Hollywood cinema collide.

Forbidden Zone cowriter Matthew Bright also played two roles in the movie. One was Squeezit the Chicken Boy, who is a nervous child in desperate need of attention and a positive role model. He spends the movie crouched in a chicken stance, waiting for approval with a look of self loathing on his face. His other part is Rene, Squeezit's transvestite brother. Rene is a prisoner in the Queen's dungeon, seeking a different kind of attention than her brother desires. Rene becomes excited by the threat of violence to the point of sexual gratification. While filming, a lighting rig came crashing onto Bright's head while he was in his Rene make up. He was taken to the emergency room with a concussion and received stitches. Upon being released, Bright reported back to the set and carried on.

After years of developing, casting, building sets by hand, shooting, and editing, *Forbidden Zone* was finally in the can—and it almost stayed there due to an unforeseen copyright issue involving Mickey Mouse ears. In the movie there are a few scenes where a large man child is seen wearing Mickey Mouse ears. One scene features Elfman's mouth superimposed over the man child's, singing a silly song. Elfman explains —

> The year was 1982. Marie [Elfman's wife at the time and who also played Frenchy] and I had just lost our house to foreclosure from *Forbidden Zone*-related loans. Three years' work, everything we owned . . . for nothing, because of fucking Mickey Mouse ears! I couldn't digest food or sleep . . . until I decided to do something about it. I decided I would find whichever

legal/accountant type at Disney was personally in charge of the "mouse ear" issue and calmly explain to him that—while I totally respect his defending his company's interests—the release of the micro-budget *Forbidden Zone* was in no possible way ever going to hurt or negatively affect the Walt Disney Company. Hadn't we covered the logo on the mouse ears? But . . . if *Forbidden Zone* never sees the light of day because of that individual's decision—and I'm *absolutely* a man of my word—it would cost him his life. It wouldn't happen right away. I'd be in Europe or somewhere when it happened. But (looking him right in the eye) he could bank on it. And with making that decision, I got my first night's sleep in a week. But I'm not a violent person at heart, and later decided I

"The whole movie was banned

didn't want something like that on my conscience, so I never ended up threatening anyone—and God must have heard my prayers because Disney ended up being very cool and didn't give us a problem. The things we do for Art! (Or fantasize doing.)

Thinking the worst of it was over, Elfman released the movie and hoped it would find its target audience. "The *whole* movie was banned from the University of Wisconsin," Elfman laments. The University decided to ban the movie because of its opening scene where a man in blackface, who, the movie notifies us is a drug dealer, is scared so deeply by the sixth dimension he flees his home (in Crenshaw). Elfman defended his choice to use a white actor in blackface even though there are black actors in the movie. "*Forbidden Zone* is a human cartoon (among other things). All the characters are over-the-top and cartoon-like. Blackface was simply more cartoon-like, more absurd. It was the absurdity I was after. In past eras, people who wished to suppress edgy art simply became righteous censors. During the '80s, they became 'politically correct'—just as righteous as the censors and just as thoroughly fucked up."

Elfman wasn't just labeled a racist, audience members also thought he was anti-Semitic. As it turns out, the man being called an anti-Semite was himself born a redheaded Jew.

The scenes that were deemed offensive were in fact acted by his Jewish grandfather, who used his regular speaking voice, and by Richard himself. "The 'Jewish' bit with my grandfather was just me taking a funny look at . . . my grandfather," says Elfman. But what about the other ambiguous religious scenes scattered

from the University of Wisconsin."

around? Some audience members were offended by Villechaize (the King) quoting the Bible the first time he sees Frenchy: "*Who is this that comes out of the wilderness like pillars of smoke, perfumed with myrrh and frankincense . . .*" "I'm not even sure who put that in the script (we had a few minor contributors besides Matthew). Elfman says, "I didn't know the verse came from the Bible until after the film was shot!" And then there was the scene where Rene the transvestite sings while hanging from a cross. "Rene on the cross was an over-the-top, absurdist way of showing her profound suffering." Were any of these jokes intentional jabs at religion, or were people reading more into them than he intended? "No joke or disrespect [was] aimed at Christians. Personally (my Hollywood secular, liberal friends notwithstanding), I think that religion does *way* more good in the world than harm. So . . . an ax to grind against religion? No. Bad taste? You betcha!"

Protests. Bomb threats. Theaters dropping the movie as if it were on fire. The human cartoon had ended before it was allowed a proper run. "The film disappeared after some scattered midnight shows in the summer of 1982. Didn't make a dime," says Elfman. It wasn't until years later that Elfman learned the movie had been bootlegged countless times and had a thriving following. "When I put my first Web site up around 2000, I got emails from all over the world. Quite a surprise! I guess it survived and expanded in the college bootleg universe. I'm still surprised to see a new generation of fans get into it. Kind of like a sick and twisted Energizer Bunny that just keeps beating it's

Protests. Bomb threats. Theaters dropping the movie as if it were on fire.

drum on and on and on . . . ." The sick and twisted Energizer Bunny is still going. The movie has seen two DVD releases in the last few years. The first release is the original black-and-white movie remastered. The second release is the version Elfman had always envisioned. It is the same cut but colorized. "My original intention was to have a colorized film (frame by frame, in China)" but the budget ran out, leaving no money for the colorization until 2008.

For diehard fans, a third release is in the works, which Elfman refers to as the "Everything and the Kitchen Sink" version. What should one expect on this third release? For starters the original 16mm footage that was eventually scrapped. There's also this warnng from Elfman: "You think *Forbidden Zone* is politically incorrect and offensive? Ha! If this ever comes out, it'll be me as well as Rene crucified up there on the cross!"

Richard Elfman is the perfect representation of an artist living his work. He is the human cartoon that he tries to recapture for the screen. And whether you like or dislike his movies, it's good to know someone is out there swimming against the stream. Not because he wants to be different, but because he is different.

You've made it through
Halloween,
now try and survive
Christmas.

SILENT NIGHT,
DEADLY NIGHT

He knows
when you've
been naughty...

TRI-STAR PICTURES PRESENTS "SILENT NIGHT, DEADLY NIGHT" LILYAN CHAUVIN GILMER McCORMICK TONI NERO
And Introducing ROBERT BRIAN WILSON as Billy Co-Executive Producers SCOTT J. SCHNEID and DENNIS WHITEHEAD
Written by MICHAEL HICKEY Produced by IRA RICHARD BARMAK Directed by CHARLES E. SELLIER, JR.
A TRI-STAR RELEASE

84012
SILENT NIGHT DEADLY NIGHT

No Cookies for Santa

9

Punish! The PTA Sends Santa off With No Cookies

ONE OF THE MOST CHERISHED HOLIDAY movies is *A Christmas Story*. The 1983 flick is a modern classic that every age group can enjoy. Utter the words, "You'll shoot your eye out!" or, "I double dog dare ya," and anyone who celebrates the holidays—hell, anyone with a pulse—will know exactly what you're talking about.

Horror nerds have their own holiday classic. You won't hear them cooing, "Every time a bill rings, an angel gets his wings." No, during the Christmas season, horror dorks deliver holiday wishes with a grunted "Punish!" or "Naughty!" It's a secret handshake of sorts.

For the uninitiated (or for those who are just too wholesome), that holiday horror classic is *Silent Night, Deadly Night*—Santa on a killing spree. The 1980s saw an explosion of "slasher" films, which featured masked men who stalk their victims until only one is left to finally strike the killer down. The slashers return from the grave only when it's financially profitable to make a sequel. Friday the 13th became associated with the character Jason Voorhees more than it did a date on the calendar. Many filmmakers were soon jumping at the chance to start their own horror franchise. By the time the decade ended just about every holiday had blood on its hands.

New Year's Eve – *New Year's Evil* 1980
Valentine's Day – *My Bloody Valentine* 1981
April Fool's Day – *April Fool's Day* 1986
Mother's Day – *Mother's Day* 1980
Halloween – *Halloween* 1978 and still going
Birthdays – *Happy Birthday to Me* 1981

In 1983, director Charles E. Sellier was approached by his good friend Ira Barmak, who had just received a green light from Tristar to turn pulp horror book *Slayride* into a celluloid moneymaker. Hesitant at first, knowing the amount of work and man-hours that go into directing, Sellier eventually agreed. *Silent Night, Deadly Night* was shot in thirty-two days with a budget of $750,000. No one on the set thought much of the movie except they were pleased at the quality of their low-budget flick. To them this was just another boogieman horror movie following the same recipe as its predecessors.

The movie is eternally goofy, and it's hard to understand how anyone could honestly be pick-up-your-placard-and-let's-go-protest upset. The story is as follows. Christmas Eve, 1971, a family is driving through a scenic mountain town on the way to visit their grandfather, who is in a hospital. Dad is driving the family station wagon, little Billy is in the back seat, and Mom is in the front passenger seat holding their younger child (who looks like a wax potato melting). Young Billy asks his parents if he can stay up late to catch a glimpse of ole Santa. His mother warns it's not a good idea but promises Santa has a big surprise for him. Hello foreshadowing!

The family arrives at the hospital where grandpa resides. Grandpa, played by Will Hare, is the best character in the whole movie. You can imagine the casting director sticking his head into a VFW hall or dive bar at two in the afternoon and saying, "Which one of you silver foxes wants to scare the hell out of a

"Which one of you silver foxes wants to

six-year-old?" Unfortunately, his role takes up a scant four or five minutes. Grandpa stares straight ahead, speechless, barely blinking, and pretending not to hear his visiting family. He's probably afraid they'll ask him to hold that ugly baby.

A doctor at the hospital asks to speak with the family out in the hall. Well, of course they're willing to speak to the doctor, but only if they can leave young, already visibly uncomfortable Billy alone with the statuesque deaf mute who stinks of whiskey and medical ointment. Wasting no time, grandpa smiles as the door closes. Billy calls for his mother, but grandpa grabs his arm as one would grab a shoplifter. Grandpa is like a spring-loaded mental patient who's been waiting years for this moment. Like any good grandparent he tells Billy that his parents can't help him and that "Christmas Eve is the scariest damn night of the year." His face contorts as if the words were excrement leaving his mouth. Oh, man, this is good stuff. Grandpa continues to quiz the child, asking if he understands, truly understands, the purpose Santa has in this world. No, he doesn't bring presents to all the boys and girls. He only brings presents to the good boys and girls. The naughty ones are punished. Billy looks like he's about to cry, and he doesn't look like he's acting.

"You see Santa Claus tonight you better run, boy! You better run for your life!" The old man wheezes, then breaks into a fit of laughter. Billy's parents return, having finished speaking with the doctor. Grandpa blinks and sits back in his chair, motionless once again, like a coin-operated fortuneteller having performed its quarter's worth.

Wow, a whole four minutes with your father on Christmas Eve! Really made that long drive over the mountain worthwhile. Even if they think the douche bag is catatonic, they could have

scare the hell out of a six-year-old?"

at least brought him a Christmas card. Billy's parents aren't evil, but they're thoughtless and self-centered. Would you bother to intervene if a man in a Santa suit tried to kill them?

Having fulfilled their family obligations, Billy and his parents make their way home in the dark. Billy begins to have a nervous breakdown, blathering every warning his grandfather shared with him. "Grandpa is nothing but a crazy old fool" Billy's mother blurts out angrily. Good thing they left their young, impressionable son alone with a crazy old fool.

While all this heartwarming holiday banter continues in the car, a man in a Santa suit is robbing a convenience store. He flees in his red sleigh, which looks like it could be a red Ford Mustang. What happens next isn't totally clear. Santa the armed felon either pulls off to the side of the road, faking car problems for the sole purpose of robbing more people who stop to help, or his car really broke down and he plans to car jack the first car that stops. These details aren't as important to the writers, who were trying to figure out how to get some titties in this flick, pronto! Of course, the parents stop to help stranded St. Nick. They're getting a kick out of the situation while Billy pleads to keep going. What the hell do kids know anyway?

This particular Santa is a

Billy's dad enquires if Santa needs help. Santa replies by shooting him in the face. Billy flees from the car and hides in the bushes only to watch his mother be pulled from the car. This particular Santa is a real piece of shit. He forces Billy's mother to the ground and begins tearing her clothes off. Then he rapes and kills her.

Fast forward to a few years later, and Billy is being raised in a Catholic orphanage. The nuns are harsh but they allow Billy to grow his mullet long and flowing. As if puberty isn't enough to deal with, Billy has confusing emotions revolving around the holidays and their true meaning. The orphanage is a cruel and confusing place too: Billy is sent to his room only to be told to go outside and play with the children a moment later.

Billy stumbles upon a couple of teenagers having sex—a superbly goofy sex scene complete with badly overdubbed moaning. Mother Superior discovers what's going on and wields a belt like Indian Jones with his whip, lashing the naked teens. She then tracks Billy down to let him know that what he has seen is "naughty" and that people who behave like that should be "punished." Then Mother Superior beats Billy's ass like Michael Vic left alone in the Humane Society for having left his room and witnessed awkward teen sex.

Having warped Billy sexually, mentally, and physically, the nuns feel they have done their job. Finally Billy turns eighteen and is free from his Catholic shackles. He lands a job in a department store where the employees seem to genuinely care for him. Then, through a series of circumstances, Billy becomes the store's Santa.

That's it. That's the set up. Once Billy is in the Santa cos-

real piece of shit.

tume, he snaps like an operative hearing his code word. Santa is on earth to punish, and now Billy is Santa. He spends the rest of the movie looking for people who are naughty and punishing them. Ever see a slasher movie? Wash, rinse, repeat, and you've seen *Silent Night, Deadly Night*. How typical is *Silent Night, Deadly Night*? Scream queen Linnea Quigley (*Graduation Day, Return of the Living Dead, Hollywood Chainsaw Hookers*, etc., you get the point) is one of the victims. There's nothing really standout except for a scene where Billy, as Santa, gives a

Mother Superior **beats Billy's ass** *like Michael Vic left alone in the Humane Society.*

"good" little girl a box cutter for Christmas. And a scene where an unarmed Santa is shot dead by a cop in front of a bunch of kids. Okay, so *Silent Night, Deadly Night* does stand out in its own way.

It's obvious *Silent Night, Deadly Night* was never picketed for content but for theme. If the movie took place on Arbor Day or Valentine's Day, where there isn't an overtly religious theme, no one would have noticed.

Silent Night, Deadly Night opened in limited release on the East Coast November 9, 1984. Three weeks later it closed, though not due to slumping ticket sales. Parents began writing letters of complaint to the media, calling the movie, "An intrusion of children's dreams and fantasies." Actor Mickey Rooney voiced his anger on the matter saying, "How dare they!" and, "The scum who made that movie should be run out of town." Rooney was quite indignant that these unthinking gore fiends had sullied the good name of Christmas . . . then he starred in *Silent Night, Deadly Night 5*: (five!) *The Toy Maker*. Irony thy name be Mickey Rooney.

The PTA (Parent Teacher Association), having solved all the problems inside public schools, weighed in, and soon adults began to picket theaters screening the offensive holiday horror.

Sellier was surprised to see the movie turned

One protest organizer wrote, "The film portends something extremely violent, something terroristic about Christmas. It's an intrusion against something we hold sacred." For the first time in history, the PTA grabbed the attention of Tristar, and *Silent Night, Deadly Night* was pulled from theaters. Director Charles Sellier believed executives decided to pull the movie before it had an impact on the studio's stocks.

To this day Sellier states he never intended to stir any controversy. In hindsight Sellier regrets having anything to do with the movie. The decision to make *Silent Night, Deadly Night* was a financial one. The movie was only meant to be a standard horror movie riding the coattails of *Friday the 13th*. No one who worked on the movie realized the anger, and free publicity, their little slasher flick would produce.

Charles Sellier is a practicing Christian. The Catholic nuns in the movie were only plot devices and never meant to be a statement about the Catholic religion. When *Silent Night, Deadly Night* had completed the editing phase, Sellier was surprised to see the movie turned out more violent than he anticipated. He now gives speeches on responsible filmmaking, using his experience on *Silent Night, Deadly Night* as an example of learning from mistakes. He only meant to make a B horror movie. He never meant to anger or offend anyone. How's that for a gift of peace?

out **more violent** *than he anticipated.*

(left) Leonardo DiCaprio; (above) Kate Winslet

TITANIC

Dude, I'm Sinking

10

Cast and Crew of *Titanic* Ride the Yellow Submarine

IN 1997 JAMES CAMERON BLURRED FACT and fiction when he released a movie called *Titanic*. The movie used the names and identities of real people who were on the fateful voyage and mixed them with a little "what if?" and "could be!" Previously, Cameron had thrilled boys of all ages with *The Terminator* in 1984. In 1991, testosterone levels all across the globe rose when he released *Terminator 2: Judgment Day*. In between the two *Terminator* movies, James Cameron made *Aliens*—arguably the best sci-fi action movie ever. So it surprised many that, after making a name for himself by creating high-octane action movies with unbelievable effects, a love story was in the works.

James Cameron had taken what he had-done for the men of the world and applied it to the gentler sex (as well as the gentler men). A love story of forbidden passion between a first-class passenger named Rose Bukater, played by Kate Winslet, and a third-class passenger named Jack Dawson, played by Leonardo DiCaprio, unfolds onscreen. Rose is upper crust, Jack is dirt poor, but full of life, and wins his cruise tickets in a card game. Once the two meet on the doomed love boat, he shows life is worth living . . . just in time to quit living.

The movie became a mega success. Women everywhere were dragging their boyfriends and husbands to the theaters—much like those boyfriends and husbands had drug their girlfriends and wives to see *Terminator 2* six years earlier. But before audiences could weep at the power of love, before James Cameron called "cut!" for the last time, even before a screeching Canadian woman bore her soul, letting the world know, yes, her heart would go on . . . there was scandal and mystery on the set of *Titanic* in 1996.

Titanic, the ship, is at the bottom of the deep sea. The cast and crew of *Titanic*, the movie, were about to be lost in the fog of Deep Purple. Steve Quale, who played one of the movie's engine room workers, comments, "Jim (James Cameron) looks around and says, 'Let's break for lunch.' We all sit down, we're eating, and suddenly it was just surreal. People we're freaking out."

Bill Paxton also noticed something unusual was happening. People were wandering around aimlessly, some were crying, others began vomiting. "One minute I felt okay," he says, "the next minute I felt so goddamn anxious I wanted to breathe in a paper bag. Cameron was feeling the same way." Fearing he had consumed a heaping bowl of bad shellfish, Paxton jumped into a car and made a bee line to the nearest hospital. Turns out the shell-fish wasn't bad. It wasn't born bad anyway . . . As Dr. Rob Roy explains: "These people were stoned."

Anyone who helped themselves to a bowl of lobster chowder during dinner service received a surprise side of PCP (scientifically known as phencyclidine), an illegal street drug that has been known to alter mood, slur speech, and cause hallucinations.

On the *Titanic* DVD, commentary producer Jon Landau speaks of the "chowder incident," recalling, "Somebody spiked our food with PCP and a large portion of our crew got sick and were taken to the hospital." Steady cam operator, Jimmy Muro, remembers, "One thirty in the morning. We have twenty hours of work to do the last day in Halifax with eight hours to go." Then, not long into their lunch break, "I'm seeing colors and fog.

"Suddenly it was just surreal.

The genius himself [James Cameron] started to feel it too. He stands up and calls for the AD and storms off the set." Eventually help arrives, and the sick are being identified. Muro continues, "Meanwhile I'm being led to a sixteen-passenger van by guys in orange suits." After being admitted into the hospital, "People [were] doing the conga line so they put us all in different rooms, and we're all sticking our heads out cause we want to be with each other. And you would hear, 'Get back in your room!'"

How did this recreational drug end up in the chowder? No one is talking, and to date the caper remains unsolved. With no obvious culprit and no witnesses, rumors began to surface. One story has a disgruntled employee of the catering company spiking the chowder. And if the employee was disgruntled, what was the purpose? To see his employer sued? The victims themselves were not ultimately responsible for the working conditions.

Earle Scott, CEO of the on-set catering company for *Titanic*, insists a member of the *Titanic* staff, not his, brought in the offending drug. "It was the Hollywood crowd bringing in the psychedelic shit." Scott told the media, "It was done like a party thing that got carried away." But if you were working on the set of *Titanic*, a major motion picture with a budget over $100 million dollars, would you risk your career for a prank?

If a staff member of the catering company wasn't responsible, and all who were working on the film were innocent, what happened? Police Sergeant Richard Hollinshead commented, "We're not even sure if it was a prank or a mistake. We're still investigating." Jeffrey Godsick, a spokesman for Twentieth Century Fox, said, "We were shocked and disturbed to learn of these results and are hopeful that the police investigation will bring

People we're freaking **out**."

those responsible to justice." The felonious merry prankster is still on the loose.

"These people were **stoned**."

CÜNEYT ARKIN

Turkish Star Wars

DÜNYAYI KURTARAN ADAM!

Remakes Through a Fever Dream Lens

11

The Turkish Film Industry Defies Copyright Laws and All Logic

BEFORE GORE VERBINSKI REMADE HIDEO Nakata's milestone horror movie, *The Ring* (or *Ringu* to all you nerds), while Donald Sutherland followed the steps of Kevin McCarthy in *Invasion of the Body Snatchers*, and before Will Smith did a better job of destroying Richard Matheson's *I Am Legend* than Charlton Heston did in *The Omega Man*, there were . . . the Turks!

Dracula is **suave** *in his own dark way.*

TARZAN IN ISTANBUL

Let's start in the year 1952 when the Turkish began their long love affair with "borrowing" themes and characters from Western cinema. The first test subject to be hurled at the largely Muslim country was Tarzan. The film was cleverly titled *Tarzan in Istanbul* and starred Tamer Balci mimicking Johnny Weissmuller, the sixth actor to play Tarzan and the first to be associated with the yodeling Tarzan yell. Scenes involving animals one would expect to see in a Tarzan film were mostly compiled from film shot at local zoos, stock footage, and scenes lifted from previous Tarzan movies. Just keep telling yourself you're seeing the African jungle and not a forest on the outskirts of Istanbul.

DRACULA IN ISTANBUL

A year later, in 1953, Mehmet Muhtar directed *Dracula in Istanbul* based on Ali Riza's 1928 book *Vlad the Impaler*, which was mostly a translation of Bram Stoker's *Dracula*. What really sets this *Dracula* apart is it's the first to show the count with the now-infamous pointy teeth. It's also the only Dracula movie not to use a crucifix (since Turkey is a Muslim country). The first and last time Dracula had belly dancers.

Still, the story stays surprisingly true to the Dracula and vampire lore we love. A necklace of garlic is used for defense. Stakes through the heart still send the damned back to their eternal slumber. Dracula is still suave in his own dark way. Like an evil Matthew McConaughey. Except Dracula keeps his shirt on. What a pimp.

Despite the low budget in *Dracula in Istanbul*, there is very little to poke fun at. Reinfeld looks like a butler on a bad '80s sitcom. A massive, and fake, Wilfred Brimley mustache takes

*Like an **evil** Matthew McConaughey.*

up much of his face. An equally fake wig sits on top of his head, cockeyed.

With the belly dancing and a scene of a woman undressing and bathing, *Dracula in Istanbul* exudes more sex than most Turkish films. Imagine the scandal the images of an unclothed woman caused in a Muslim country in 1952.

What is clear is this is an attempt to recreate the scares and atmosphere of Todd Browning's *Dracula*. Somebody saw the original, and it left such an impression that they put in effort to tell the same story while adapting some tweaks for their own culture. It's not the slapped-together mess we see in *Turkish Wizard of Oz* or *Badi* the *Turkish E.T.* (more about them in a moment).

The use of zoom, focus, and light shows creativity and understanding of what makes a good vampire movie. Definitely worth a curious look for fans of the genre or the golden age of the silver screen. While not the definitive bloodsucker flick, it is leaps and bounds better than a number of its American contemporaries.

His crotch wig swings wildly, even

TURKISH *WIZARD OF OZ*

In 1971 Tunc Basaran started a cold war against one of America's most valued films and favorite movie-going memories. He remade *The Wizard of Oz*. Its long and cumbersome title translates to *Little Ayse and the Magic Dwarfs in the Land of Dreams*. Really rolls off the tongue, doesn't it? No expense is spared when the tornado strikes "Kansas" in the Turkish version of *The Wizard of Oz*. A poorly animated tornado picks up the house and slowly moves it from left to right across the screen. Dorothy/Ayse isn't even animated. A paper cutout of her also moves slowly from one side of the screen to the other. When the house lands, Dorothy/Ayse opens her eyes, and she is immediately dancing with dwarfs dressed as nutcrackers. No segue, no introduction to the Lollipop Guild, no yellow brick road to be seen. She's in the house and then she's dancing. There are no ruby slippers but she does find silver ones (silver spray paint must be cheaper) next to the house . . . no witch or curling legs though. Every character is either highly effeminate or slightly threatening when they're not supposed to be. The cowardly lion has mange. His costume is a body suit with a mane on his head and a wig on his crotch. His crotch wig swings wildly, even dragging the ground on occasion. The Wizard of Oz also turns out to be Merlin. That guy is everywhere. Also, Kansas and Oz look oddly like Turkey. Oh, yeah, and there is a caveman fight scene. What did we ever do to Turkey?

3 MIGHTY MEN

In 1973 director Fikret Ucak brought us *3 Mighty Men*. The film revolves around a villain in one of the worst superhero costumes

dragging the ground on occasion.

worn by man or child. You know a movie is either going to be amazing or terrible when it opens with a man wearing a Spiderman costume, and his giant, bushy, black eyebrows are sticking out of the mask holes. Spidey and his henchmen bury a woman up to her neck in sand, then cut her head off with a boat motor. This is in the first two minutes of the movie. Then the credits roll like a bad slide show acid trip. The actors hold unnatural poses in the still as they pull away from the screen.

We jump back to the movie where men in paisley lounge suits discuss important things. Then Spiderman jumps out of pile of wood and stabs a man to death. A woman is kidnapped and tied to a pole with twine. Then Captain America shows up to save the woman. Except . . . Captain America is . . . Turkish. A nonsensical fight breaks out, spills into a graveyard, and ends with Spiderman dragging Captain America alongside a car.

The very next scene shows Santo, the famous Mexican wrestler (aka *luchador*), rummaging through some guy's office. He's sticking things down his wrestling pants and kicking the crap out of random people who cross his path. This might be the best way to explain it: Let's say you see a child playing with toys that don't go together, like GI Joe and Transformers. Yet in this child's mind, these toys exist in the same universe, and they may have different duties than originally intended. So the only thing that could make sense is if a Turkish *child* wrote this movie.

Other points of interest include: Spiderman choking a woman to death in the shower; Spiderman sending rats down a tube to eat a man's face; an incredibly unseductive dance number by silhouette; a man who looks like a Turkish Charles Bronson stunt

Take a drink every time a man with a mustache is

double; Spiderman impaling two people together in the shower (what's with the shower killing?); a fight scene complete with a silly wind-machine gag.

Don't watch this one sober.

TURKISH *STAR TREK*

Also released in 1973 was a film called *Omer the Tourist in Star Trek*. This is another lift of musical score, characters, and ideas placed into an original Turkish story. Omer is a hobo and unwilling groom at a shotgun wedding. Then for unknown reasons (no subtitles are provided), Omer is transported onto the Starship Enterprise. Omer also has a striking resemblance to Steve Martin's character "the wild and crazy guy."

Once transported, (Turkish) Spock, (Turkish) Kirk, the newly freed groom, and the rest of the Star Trek cast hang out with gold-painted women and a really homoerotic robot wearing nothing but a leopard-print Speedo. The bulk of the movie takes place on the ship's deck, which means there isn't much to follow unless you know the language. What is clear is there is a shape-shifting creature who can assume a person's identity by touching their face then tasting its hand. Yep. These creatures, when not taking the form of a victim, look like dollar store Morlocks from 1960's *Time Machine*. These monsters have two forms of attack: They hold their arms up in the air and scream, or they try to touch your face and taste their hands. It goes without saying that once discovered, they're easily overthrown.

It also goes without saying that *Omer the Tourist in Star Trek* has a very small budget. The sound effect for doors opening and closing on the Enterprise is simply someone making a "swish" sound with their mouth. Spock's ears are more fake than Pamela

on screen. You'll be drunk before the second act.

Anderson's breasts. His plastic Vulcan ears are clearly a different skin tone than the rest of Spock (or as he's known in this movie, "Spak"). They're just half-assed sitting on top of the actor's real ears.

Before the movie is finally over, and you're allowed to cry, the movie pulls a few more fastballs. The climax comes when the homoerotic robot comes to life and dives into a slap fight with other homoerotic robots in leopard-print Speedos. None of this makes sense, but it doesn't really matter . . . it actually enhances the viewing pleasure of this movie.

In the end, the greaseball is returned to his shotgun wedding. The bride is shocked to see her groom returned and more shocked to find he now has Vulcan ears. The groom, seeing a way out of marriage to an ugmo, performs the Vulcan death grip on his would-be in-laws and escapes single to live another day.

For being a low-budget rip-off, *Omer the Tourist in Star Trek* has the most heart and seems to understand its source material better than the other Turkish "remakes." The costumes and overall feel of the crew, as well as the Enterprise itself, are as close as any American fanboy could make.

SEYTAN AKA TURKISH *EXORCIST*

Jump to 1974 when Metin Erksan dared to make an almost scene-for-scene remake of William Friedkin's *The Exorcist* called *Seytan*. If you haven't started doing drugs yet, now's a good time to start. William Peter Blatty wrote what has to be the most famous piece of modern horror fiction, *The Exorcist*—the tale of a child tormented by an evil entity. In 1973 the wave of success William Friedkin was riding from directing *The French Connection* (1971) was about to grow threefold, having completed a film adaptation of Blatty's book, also called *The Exorcist*. Wast-

"The bed vibrates like a Magic

ing no time, the Turkish film industry tossed a man named Metin Erksan behind the camera to direct *Seytan* in 1974. Even Mike Oldfield's instantly recognizable score, "Tubular Bells," makes numerous appearances. The Turkish version of *The Exorcist* is entertaining—but for all the wrong reasons.

Seytan is almost an exact copy of *The Exorcist*. The "rats" are in the attic; there's an architectural dig with scary and ominous artifacts; (Turkish) Father Karras has a sick mother (who looks like she's on her way to a Harry Potter convention); (Turkish) Regan shows her mother how she talks to Captain Howdy through a Ouija board . . . except now he's known as Captain Ler-sen. And, of course, the bed still shakes (obviously people pushing from below.)

What makes *Seytan* more interesting than some of its rip-off colleagues is what has been altered. "Father Karras" isn't a priest in this version . . . he's a psychiatrist. The guilt he feels for his mother is because she panhandled to pay for his schooling. "Regan" is treated as mentally ill and not possessed by an entity. When the mother seeks out a priest, she ends up finding the psychiatrist to help rid her child of her unwanted tenant. An exorcism is performed only when the psychiatrist feels it will work because the sick child will believe in it. No Christian symbolism is found throughout the movie.

Also, "Regan" is still an angry and violent little girl, but she lacks the full-fledged sailor tongue of her American counterpart. No one's mother sucks cocks in hell. The crucifix masturbation scene is missing. *Seytan*'s bluest moments occur when the young girl occasionally calls someone a bastard.

Providing the most hilarity is a scene where doctors say

Fingers hotel bed gone wild."

they'd like to check the spinal chord of the disturbed child and maybe even do shock therapy to get the lass back to normal. Cut to a close-up shot of the little girl's head stuck in what looks like a paint-can mixer and paper towels in her mouth. Was her spinal chord damaged? It is now!

The exorcism finally comes, complete with all the spit takes. The bed vibrates like a Magic Fingers hotel bed gone wild. In the blink of an eye the bedroom looks like the opening act to an Ozzy Osborne concert. "Father Merrin" swallows an Altoid and dies. When "Kerras" finds the body, he flips out and begins beating the possessed child with his bare fists. Believe it or not, the final scene of *Seytan* is a grown man punching a child repeatedly before jumping to his death.

TURKISH *YOUNG FRANKENSTEIN*

Remaking *E.T.*, *Star Wars*, or *Rambo* makes sense. These movies were big hits in the United States and have worked their way into the pop culture lexicon. But Mel Brooks? And if it has to be Mel Brooks, why not *Blazing Saddles*? How funny would it be to see the over-the-top racial humor of *Blazing Saddles* translated into the Turkish language?

Mel Brooks and Gene Wilder combined forces in 1974 and wrote the comedic adaptation of Mary Shelley's *Frankenstein*. A Turkish screen writer named Nejat Saydam enjoyed *Young Frankenstein* so much he stole the concept, jokes, and characters to make his own version. The Turks have lifted the soundtrack from the original film, and the story stays remarkably faithful to the source material. To a degree. *Turkish Young Frankenstein* wavers

Badi just shows up at the kids' home, kicks the

somewhere between shot for shot and total bastardization. All the scenes are there; however, new "jokes" are occasionally inserted. For example, Dr. Frankenstein dressed up as the monster, squirting water from his nipples. Why? Why not?

As a side note, if you find yourself in possession of these Turkish remakes try to keep track of how many mustaches get screen time. Or if you're a lush, make a drinking game out of it. Take a drink every time a man with a mustache is on screen. You'll be drunk before the second act.

The Turkish replacement for Gene Wilder looks like a used car salesmen. The replacement for Terri Gar has zero charisma. The replacement for Marty Feldman lacks any physical characteristics or ability for physical acting. The entire package is so close to being a carbon copy and yet would rate even lower than a high school production.

The director decides to further confuse the viewers by filming multiple day for night scenes. At first glance, it seems these shots are intended to take place during the day . . . until you notice the characters are holding candlesticks. *Dracula in Istanbul* figured out night shooting twenty years prior. Is the Turkish film industry devolving?

BADI AKA TURKISH *E.T.*

In 1982 Steven Spielberg won the hearts and minds of American children when he released *E.T.: The Extra-Terrestrial*. In 2005 Spielberg trampled his own movie (much like George Lucas with his *Star Wars* re-releases) by replacing dialog, using computers to replace guns with walkie talkies, and inserting a CGI (computer-generated imagery) E.T. that looked less lifelike and more bizarre than the original E.T. puppet. Before Spielberg or Lucas could

door open, and blasts a giant smoke-machine fart.

declare, "It may be your childhood but it's my movie!" the Turkish raped the franchise in 1983—only a year after the original was released.

Badi was the international answer to the question *E.T.: The Extra-Terrestrial* never asked. There are no subtitles to *Badi*, so here is what you might be able to gather. The movie starts off with three children who look prematurely aged by years of alcohol abuse and tobacco. They're setting fire to various powders on the kitchen table, causing numerous explosions.

A schoolmaster kicks a dog. The dog gets a brief vacation on a camping trip. (Perhaps as some sort of reward for the abuse?) Then the dog is found dead in the street. Let's face it, no children's movie is complete without a scene of a dead dog being thrown on the back of a pickup by its lifeless legs. This all happens within the first ten minutes of the movie. Sweet dreams, kids!

E.T. looked like a shaved Walter Matthau left out in the sun. Badi looks like someone microwaved a turd.

The Turkish city in which *Badi* takes place looks about as inviting as Flint, Michigan, after GM left town. All the buildings and homes looked bombed out. It's hard to imagine *Badi* did anything to help promote tourism to Turkey.

Then there's the whole storytelling issue with the adults. With the exception of Elliott's mother, *E.T.: The Extra-Terrestrial* was careful not reveal the adults in the children's lives until they were shown as unintentional villains who come close to causing the alien's demise. *Badi* has no sense of mystery or use of visual cues to make the children central figures of the story. Adults are everywhere, and they're often beating the children.

E.T. arrived to California full of wonder at seeing a new planet. Badi arrives to Turkey, his papier-mâché head tilting to

Not having the budget for special effects is one

one side, and the movie cuts back to a father chasing his son with what looks like a tire iron. The children of this household don't seem to be related to our Turkish "Elliott," but they're getting more screen time than anyone else.

There are no trails of Reese's Pieces. There is no childhood innocence as Elliott attempts to befriend a mysterious visitor. Badi just shows up at the kids' home, kicks the door open, and blasts a giant smoke-machine fart. Badi and his second string Elliottt quickly become friends. Maybe this is a cultural thing, or it could be the language barrier, but the alien feeds the boy cake, and they may be married now.

Which brings us to the alien itself. The American E.T. was reluctantly adorable. You couldn't help but love him even though he looked like a shaved Walter Matthau left out in the sun. Badi is just gross. No one could love him. He not only appears to be mentally impaired, but he looks like someone microwaved a turd. Steven Spielberg created a story where a child shows love and compassion for a lost and misunderstood creature. Spielberg's Turkish counterparts created a story where a boy is in love with a dirty alien.

Badi is simply a dwarf wearing a body sock. A body sock that strangely has tits, genitals that emit smoke, and a head whose unblinking eyes barely stay attached to the costume. Not having the budget for special effects is one thing, but the inability to entertain is another.

E.T. sees a romantic scene on television. Badi reads smutty porn magazines.

Elliott and E.T. make their getaway on flying bicycles, truly an iconic moment in American filmmaking. Badi and the neighborhood children escape on a flying cart stolen from a merchant.

thing, but the inability to entertain is another.

Maybe the children of Turkey don't have bicycles. They also have no problem robbing elderly cart venders of the very thing they need to make a living.

It seems only fair that America should remake *Badi*.

VAHSI KAN AKA TURKISH *RAMBO*

First Blood was a campy action movie that wanted to show viewers the obstacles veterans faced after war while providing roughly one thousand explosions at the same time. Turkish *Rambo* wanted to show viewers how many explosives five dollars can buy.

In 1982 two-time Academy Award nominee Sylvester Stallone played a troubled young man who no longer fit in society in *First Blood*. Brian Dennehy played a villainous sheriff who rejects anything he doesn't deem savory. Even a young David Caruso has a supporting role and manages to not be supported by the use of sunglasses. Wasting no time, the Turks released *Vahsi Kan* aka Turkish *Rambo* in 1983 with hilarious results. It opens with the "Kunt Film" logo displayed as goons enter a freewheeling party, beating the ever-loving crap out of every man and woman indiscriminately. Cut to people being pistol whipped, set on fire, panty shots, and what is either zombies or cannibals raping/eating a woman. So far no resemblance to Rambo. Unlike Turkish

The scenario is more confusing than

E.T. or Turkish *Wizard of Oz*, this is not a literal translation. *Vahsi Kan* doesn't start as a literal translation anyway.

Our Rambo character is soon seen walking alone down a lonely road. Turns out, our leading man is none other than Cuneyt Arkin, the star of Turkish *Star Wars*. Cuneyt attempts to fill the boots Stallone wore in *First Blood*. The biggest problem is Cuneyt is not physically intimidating—chewing on a match is his only tough guy move. Instead of being stopped and harassed by the local sheriff, this Rambo is taunted by local ruffians on motorbikes, which whiz around and around while the same five-second sound effect is looped. Rambo is held captive by these bikers. Just as in the original, Rambo is stripped of his trademark knife. Moments later when Rambo should be on the receiving end of forced grooming, the goons pull out knives and cut our hero. The scenario is more confusing than a David Lynch crossword puzzle.

Like American Rambo, Turkish "Rambo" jumps from a cliff side, but the helicopter is missing. Turkish "Rambo" hides under brush, but he comes off as pathetic instead of menacing. American Rambo kills and eats a wild pig. Turkish "Rambo" kills and eats a wild crab. Having had his fill of crab, "Rambo" uses his necktie as a headband, setting the traps for his rotten-toothed foes.

Also not in the original *First Blood* is some sort of leader of the villains who is missing both arms from the elbows down. His tirades and flailing half limbs make him look like a demented finger puppet. Then you notice that the man's arms are just tucked up in his sleeves. Like he is doing the chicken dance . . . really. Really.

a David Lynch crossword puzzle.

Vahsi Kan is missing the tones of nationalism, but the movie does give our hero a love interest. She attempts to flirt, showing nipple while bathing in a stream, but "Rambo" is not interested in these things. He hands his lady a halter top and short shorts (how did he make these clothes?), then takes off into the wild, imitating a bush and killing random men for a loaf of bread. Cuneyt Arkin dressed as a bush killing people would feel more natural in a Monty Python script than *Rambo*. It's just silly.

Obviously, *Vahsi Kan* is unable to incorporate into the story the themes of the Vietnam War and the treatment of soldiers returning from war. Without knowing the language, it's hard to determine what all the bad blood is about. Turkish "Rambo" is the only male without a mustache in this movie . . . so maybe he broke some Turkish mustache law.

TURKISH *STAR WARS*

The Turks did remake *Star Wars*, and it is terrible, but they beat George Lucas to the punch of making the first truly lousy Star Wars movie by seventeen years. Cuneyt Arkin, who later would play Turkish Rambo, steps into frame this time as a Turkish Luke Skywalker. Cuneyt looks more like an uncle who had too much to drink at a Fourth of July barbecue than he does a young, charismatic hero, as he reenacts (poorly and inaccurately) all his favorite scenes from four different movies.

After watching Turkish Star Wars, *you* **might** *be tempted to ingest*

Lets go through a brief checklist of what Turkish *Star Wars* has to offer—

- Scenes (actual footage) lifted directly from the first *Star Wars* movie
- A Darth Vader villain who looks more like Emperor Ming from Flash Gordon
- Soundtrack lifted directly from *Indiana Jones*
- Alien/Muppet costumes made out of scrap carpet
- Robot choking small child to death
- The film's hero jumping on boulders like a trampoline

Turkish *Star Wars* isn't just bad, it's spectacularly bad. It is torture worse than waterboarding. Worse than having John Tesh as a neighbor while he practices relentlessly before a tour. No one seems to know what's going on or what the story is. The characters talk, look confused, jump around, with actual footage from the first *Star Wars* movie spliced in. The theme from

Indiana Jones is played randomly to confirm that, in fact, you are in hell.

Turkish *Star Wars* is a confusing and cheaply thrown together mess. Obviously, you have to track this down and watch it. After watching it, though, you might be tempted to ingest more booze and drugs than Carrie Fisher did in the '80s.

more *booze and drugs than Carrie Fisher did in the '80s.*

Three Die Under Shocking Circumstances

12

No Redemption

ℬ ℭ

THE TWILIGHT ZONE THE TELEVISION SHOW
was a stepping-stone for some actors like Dennis Hopper, Lee Marvin, Carol Burnett, Charles Bronson, and Robert Redford. *Twilight Zone: The Movie* put an end to not just the careers but also the lives of one actor and two children.

In 1982, John Landis was a shooting star, having directed hit movies such as *Animal House* and *The Blues Brothers*. The budget for *The Blues Brothers* was the biggest he'd ever had to work with, and then he exceeded that budget by millions. The car chases aspired to be faster than previously seen in films like *Bullitt* or *The French Connection*. When the stunt drivers were ordered to drive even faster, script supervisor, Katherine Wooten, suggested reducing the camera's frames per second for the same effect. Landis refused saying, "I just want them to go faster!" When another scene called for an explosion, Landis rejected using black powder despite safety warnings from his crew. He insisted on using dynamite so he could capture an even larger explosion on camera. The resulting detonation was so big it damaged a nearby church.

"I just want them to go faster!"

John Landis had achieved his dream of becoming a director, and just like Ray Harryhausen who inspired him so many years earlier, he wouldn't be happy unless the finished product wasn't just a movie but an experience.

Earlier in his career, Landis's path had crossed with another young up-and-comer named Steven Spielberg. The two became friends, sharing the same vision of movies being grandiose experiences. Though critically panned, *The Blues Brothers* was a financial success. And while he wasn't held in the same regard as his friend Steven Spielberg, Landis was known for being able to turn a profit. So when Spielberg had the opportunity to make a movie version of the iconic television series *The Twilight Zone*, he contacted Landis to direct one of the film's segments.

The segment John Landis had control over for *Twilight Zone: The Movie* would be the only one with a totally original story.

The other segments would be retellings of episodes aired during the show's initial run. The story may have been freshly penned, but it still had many of the trademarks that made *The Twilight Zone* famous. The main character is a man named Bill Connor, an unlikable, prejudiced man who shouted bigoted remarks.

The first draft of the script had Bill suddenly being a black male pursued by the Ku Klux Klan, then a Jewish man in danger of being sent to a death camp, and then finally a Vietnamese man under attack by American soldiers. The story was not only controversial for lumping American soldiers in the same group as Nazis and Klan members, but the Bill character was so unlikable that the studio felt no audience would care about his struggle.

After some thought, Landis agreed, and also saw an opportunity to construct his biggest explosion yet. In the new draft, the

If young John Landis had any fear for

story hits a fever pitch when character Bill Connor picks up two Vietnamese children and rushes them to safety as a helicopter strafes them with bullets. The story failed to end in an ironic twist, a staple of *The Twilight Zone* episodes, but explosions on screen would make up for that—and in the end the children are safe, and Bill Connor learns the error of his way.

The second draft of the script was an improvement, although a new problem had emerged. The scene had potential to be very dangerous and called for night filming. Even if fears of small children being in close proximity to low-flying helicopters and explosions could be quelled, they would never be allowed to film into the night. The decision was made that since the children wouldn't have speaking roles, they were extras and not actors. Once willing parents were located, the "extras" would be paid in petty cash, keeping them off payroll books and not needing to sign contracts.

Finding child actors was one part of the equation. The other part was finding someone to play the role of Bill Connor. Obtaining an A-list actor would be difficult since the budget was smaller than what Spielberg or Landis were used to working with. Nevertheless, Landis liked the idea of using a lesser-known actor and keeping the directors the stars of the show. Landis's knowledge of film was more useful than a Rolodex, and he used it to brainstorm possible leading men. Vic Morrow had more than enough experience playing hard-edged men and soldiers in his career. Also, Morrow was ecstatic to have the opportunity to work on a major motion picture after years of playing in B movies and made-for-television movies.

Filming began, and, like any project of this size, filming did not always run smoothly. If young John Landis, who was riding

his cast and crew, he did not show it.

a wave of success, had any fear for his cast and crew, he did not show it. When one scene using blanks didn't provide desired results, live ammunition was used. The practice was unheard of, and many were stunned. Another scene called for Vic Morrow's character to run across a ledge thirty feet high. Landis insisted on not using a stunt double so close-up shots could be achieved. To make matters even more dangerous, Morrow was running across the ledge with no safety harness and no airbags below. While cameras rolled, Landis would shout for Morrow to run faster. Had he fallen, there was nothing to stop him but the pavement.

Other accounts have Landis screaming for someone who wasn't too "chicken shit" to get the job done. And again when one of the effects crew expressed concern over the chopper scene, Landis shot back, "Well, we may lose the helicopter." Everything on the set seemed to be a dangerous mixture of chaos and stress.

Finishing touches to the final scene were happening in rapid motion. Helicopter pilot Dorcey Wingo surveyed the set before nightfall to familiarize himself with the terrain and address any possible dangers. Wingo was not the first choice to pilot the chopper in the dangerous scene, but he did have experience flying in Vietnam and as a personal pilot. Previous candidates had turned the offer down due to the low pay and the director's persistence to sacrifice safety precautions for realism. For Wingo, who was trying to break into flying stunt choppers in the movies, this was the opportunity he was waiting for. He warned not to actually blow up the huts in the village and to not allow any of the pyrotechnics to come too close to his craft. He warned any debris could be sucked into the rotors and cause the helicopter to crash. He was also eager to please not just Landis but Spielberg as well, hoping a job well done would mean more work.

the main rotor hits water and a massive

The date was July 23, 1982. It was the final day of filming for Landis's section of the movie. The earlier shot hadn't gone smoothly. The helicopter had flown in for the establishing shots. One of the explosions had gone off too close to the helicopter, spraying water across the windshield and rocking it violently. The pilot, cameramen, and members of the effects crew again voiced concerns of the proximity and size of the explosions.

The cast and crew were anxious to get the final, most dangerous shot complete. Six cameras rolled at six different angles when "Action!" was shouted and everyone scrambled to fulfill their part of the shoot. With bullhorn in hand, Landis shouts, "Lower! Lower! Lower! Fire! Fire! Fire!" Vic Morrow runs through the water as fast as he is capable with a child under each arm. Explosions erupt all around the set, one so strong that, for a moment, the film turns into a blinding white light; the helicopter flies through the scene from right to left. Morrow loses his footing, half falling, but keeping a hold of the children. The helicopter enters the shot again but this time out of control, spinning in circles and crashing to the ground. In seconds it's over; the main rotor hits water and a massive spray cuts through the night sky. What was moving at the pace of an amusement park ride is now as still as a snapshot.

The parents of the children screamed out in terror. Renee Shin-Yi was crushed underneath the skid of the helicopter. Myca Dinh Le and Vic Morrow had been decapitated by the helicopter's main rotor. Some of the cast and crew became physically ill while others went into shock. A voice came over a loud speaker, "That's a wrap!" then ordered everyone off the set and to go home. Police arrived on set not much later.

The sun was beginning to rise, police were taking statements,

spray **cuts through** *the night sky*

and those injured in the crash and fireballs were sent to the hospital. Among the injured sent to the hospital was John Landis, who placed a phone call to his attorney. Within the hour he was admitted and discharged.

A criminal investigation was opened as well as an investigation by the NTSB (National Transportation Safety Board). The NTSB closed the case before providing any definitive answers.

Warner Bros. Studio and Steven Spielberg immediately tried to distance themselves from John Landis and his contribution to *Twilight Zone: The Movie*. Warner Bros. stressed that Spielberg and Landis were the heads of the project and that no executive was aware of the illegal hiring. Spielberg refused to speak publicly on the matter, severing ties with Landis as fast as possible. When Warner Bros. decided that not finishing the project would appear to be an admission of guilt, directors Steven Spielberg,

Joe Dante, and George Miller were notified to film their segments. Spielberg remained hesitant but was reminded that he was contractually obligated to deliver his portion of the film. Reluctantly, he filmed the "Kick the Can" segment in six days.

In a move that left many wondering what their true motives were, John Landis and George Folsey Jr., the producer who knowingly hired the two youngest victims illegally, attended the funeral for Vic Morrow. Morrow's long-time friend Steve Shagan confronted the two, who said they had prepared eulogies. Shagan found their words inappropriate and began screaming at Folsey, "Why don't you just run the trailer?!"

Landis also attended the funeral for Renee Shin-Yi, where he placed a flower on the young girl's casket. The funeral for Myca Dinh Le was held after Shin-Yi's. Landis appeared at this funeral as well, where he received many glares from the victim's family. But Landis might have been criticized for not attending the funeral just as he was for attending.

In the meantime, CAL/OSHA performed their own investigation on Landis's set. What they found were thirty-six safety violations, and what they recommended was for the Los Angeles County district attorney to pursue criminal prosecutions. CAL/OSHA felt there was a strong case for violation of the labor code and manslaughter. On June 15, 1983, a grand jury delivered indictments of manslaughter against John Landis, George Folsey Jr., Dorsey Wingo, special effects crew member Paul Stewart, and unit production manager Dan Allingham.

A pretrial ensued, with the defense hoping the judge would dismiss the case. The prosecution called in a scientist to testify that debris from an exploding hut had interfered with the helicopter and caused the crash. The defense called their own expert who claimed that heat from one of the explosions damaged the tail rotor and caused the crash. The exact cause of the crash may seem insignificant, but the defense argued that the defendants could not have predicted the crash since there are no other documented cases of "heat delamination." The prosecution retorted that, documented or not, no one on the crew used common sense— "A fireball is a fireball is a fireball." On April 23, 1984, the pretrial came to an end. The judge gave his verdict, "This court believes that a crime, to wit, involuntary manslaughter was in fact committed." Landis told the awaiting press outside, "It is disheartening to learn that being innocent is not enough."

After the pretrial the defense ran out of appeals and a lengthy jury selection followed. The defense had no option but to face the charges in court along with possible jail time. It was the first time a director had faced criminal charges for an on-set accident. The prosecutor painted a vivid picture of the violent special effects Landis had planned and the expert pilot as well as the expert effects artist who allowed it to happen despite their own grave fears and warnings. The defense claimed the tragic event

"A fireball is a fireball is a fireball."

an unforeseeable accident. An accident that was part act of God and part carelessness from the effects operator who set off the explosions. The operator in question was James Camomile, who obtained immunity in exchange for his testimony for the prosecution.

The prosecution began bringing out their witnesses, seventy-one in all, including a secretary who had conversations with Landis and Folsey, acknowledging the illegal hiring of children. The secretary testified that Folsey had even commented to her, "[If] they find out about the explosives, then they'll throw my butt in jail." The defense rebutted by pointing out that the secretary had never mentioned Folsey's damning statement in any other questioning before. Therefore it was unreliable at best or perjury at worst. There was also the child welfare worker who testified that permits would not have been issued not just because of the late hour but also the proximity of explosives and the low-flying helicopter near the children. Then all four parents of the two slain children spoke under oath: they were told that the only concern they should have would be the late hour of filming. There had been no mention of the helicopter or fireball explosions. To this the defense claimed (in an act record-breaking bad taste) the parents were motivated by money in their pending civil suite. The firemen who worked on the set, as is necessary when working with explosives, were sworn in. Their collective testimony had Landis shouting irrationally at crew members followed by the largest explosion any of the men had seen. Furthermore, the permits issued were not followed. To this the defense rebutted that, as experts, the firemen should

"We're all going to wind up in jail"

have halted all filming once their concerns arose. Following the firemen were a slew of set designers, stunt men, effects artists, and finally James Camomile (the effects operator with immunity), who admitted to not seeing the position of the helicopter while he fired the explosions.

Finally the defense team had their opportunity to speak. After the barrage of accusations, it was decided John Landis would be their first witness. The move was partly an attempt to tell his side of the story and partly an attempt to show he was not the screaming monster portrayed by prosecutors. Once Landis was sworn in, the defense went to great lengths to stress that his script was a moral story of racial tolerance. Landis acknowledged he broke the child labor laws but had every intention of keeping the children safe, saying, "We would honor not the letter of the law but the spirit of the law." Having felt Mr. Landis had established himself as a moral and careful person, he then denied everything the prosecutors and their witnesses had testified against him. He denied he received any warnings the scene was too dangerous and claimed he notified the parents of the slain children how the scene would be filmed and what to expect. He denied the use of live ammunition on set and denied he ever said, "We're all going to wind up in jail" if caught.

One would think having Landis testify would be the wild card but things got wilder when Gary Kesselman was called to testify. Kesselman was the prosecuting attorney during the grand jury and pretrial. However, a scandal involving a club in which he was partial owner and prostitution caused him to have to walk away. The defense called Kesselman because he claimed the current prosecutor, Lea D'Agostino, asked him to "remember" aspects of testimony he couldn't recall. Under cross-examination Kesselman would only say he didn't feel threatened by D'Agostino but pressured. He explained that his decision to testify for the defense was an effort to salvage his reputation and integrity from the previous scandal.

In another surprise move, helicopter pilot Darcy Wingo took the stand in his own defense. His testimony of knowing the placement of the explosives contradicted previous statements he had given the NTSB. Wingo blamed these inconsistencies on PTSD (post traumatic stress disorder). The testimony supplied to the NTSB was inaccurate, and it wasn't until seeing the accident footage that he was able to regain his complete memory of the night the accident happened. The testimony he was providing now was complete and accurate.

Several other experts were called in to testify that the helicopter crashed due to heat delamination. Again, not only were there no other reported cases of heat delamination, but the pyrotechnic that caused the accident was fired by James Camomile. The defense would argue that the real culprit could not be brought to justice since he was given immunity so prosecutors could hunt bigger game.

After hearing countless witnesses, seeing the accident from all six filmed angles, and visiting the scene of the accident, the jury would determine if the five defendants were guilty of manslaughter. In closing statements, the prosecutor called Landis and Wingo liars whose only defense was blaming other people and throwing up technical smokescreens. The defense in their own statements concluded the prosecution and their witnesses had so many lies of their own that Gary Kesselman had to be called in. They also made sure to drive home that it was wrong and careless to hire the two children illegally, but that was not the reason for the trial. After nine days of deliberating, the jury came back with a verdict. Not guilty. The nine-month trial was over. John Landis thanked the jury for using common sense. In an interview, prosecutor Lea D'Agostino said the jury had made a serious mistake. While the defendants would not be punished by the judicial system, she knew they would eventually answer to a higher power.

Who's to blame? It would be easy to put it on John Landis. After all, he was the director, the man put in charge to see the project got finished on time, on budget, and without catastrophe. However, there was an entire crew who allowed the accident to happen. Special effects supervisors who should have refused to allow unsafe pyrotechnics to happen. There was the pilot who saw the potential for disaster but pushed ahead in an attempt to further his career. Perhaps more culpable was George Folsey Jr., the producer who actively sought out two children for an illegal and dangerous night shoot. Whatever their reasons, the cogs that made up the crew allowed this to happen as much as John Landis did.

When *Twilight Zone: The Movie* was finally released, reviews were lukewarm, citing that too much attention was spent on special effects and not enough on the story. *The Twilight Zone*, the television show, was low budget and dependent on structure, story, and an actor's ability to bring chills. *Twilight Zone: The Movie* was made in an era when special effects were advancing, and, unfortunately, the directors failed to realize that bigger isn't always better.

NO SEQUELS:

Brief Stories

of Actors Who

No Longer

Need

Agents

13

Swan Songs:
Celebrity Suicides

භා ශ්

WE LIVE IN A CELEBRITY-CRAZED CULTURE
where movie stars are placed high upon ped-
estals simply because they are movie stars. In
the public's mind, they are superhuman. So, it
is a shocking blow when one of them commits
the unthinkable. It's in these sobering moments
when the curtain falls, and for just a brief moment, we all seem to be one thing—human.

PEG ENTWISTLE

Peg Entwistle was born Millicent Lillian Entwistle, February 5, 1908. She would later change her name to Peg when she started her acting career. In 1916 the Entwistle family moved from London to New York, where her father worked as a stage manager.

She began stage acting in 1925, working her way up to Broadway, obtaining critical acclaim. Actress Bette Davis claimed that once she saw Peg Entwistle play Hedvig in *The Wild Duck*, she knew she wanted to be an actress and would one day play the character Hedvig as well. In 1932 Peg traveled to act in a play called *The Mad Hopes*. Peg's performance was so impressive she was asked to stay in Los Angeles after the play's run and perform a screen test for RKO Pictures. After signing a one-picture contract, she filmed scenes to appear in the movie *Thirteen Women*.

Once *Thirteen Women* was completed, it was shown to test audiences and received mostly negative feedback. The studio held back the release of the movie in order for a second round of editing to occur. The run time of *Thirteen Women* was slashed, and Peg Entwistle had her screen time reduced drastically. Peg's romance with the silver screen was fleeting, and RKO chose not to renew her contract.

"I am afraid, I am a coward. I am sorry . . ."

Despondent and depressed, Peg told her uncle, who she was living with at the time, that she was going out for a walk. Her walk led up a steep hill, which was home to the famous Hollywood sign (however, in 1932 the sign still read Hollywoodland). Leaving her coat carefully folded along with a note, Peg used a service ladder to climb to the fifty feet to the top of the letter "H" and leapt to her death. The note she left behind read, "I am afraid, I am a coward. I am sorry for everything. If I had done this a long time ago, it would have saved a lot of pain. P.E."

September 16, 1932 Peg Entwistle left this world at just twenty-four years old but lives on in infamy as "The Hollywood Sign Girl."

GEORGE SANDERS

He worked with Alfred Hitchcock, won an Academy Award, and has two stars on the Hollywood Walk of Fame. George Sanders accomplished more than most of us ever will, but success apparently didn't keep him content. Before beginning his life as an entertainer, George Sanders held a straight job in an advertising agency. It was on the encouragement from a secretary that he pursued an acting career.

George's film debut was in the 1929 film *Strange Cargo*. His new vocation progressed in the 1930s as he appeared in over a dozen movies. In 1940 he achieved an honor many attempted to obtain by landing a supporting role in *Rebecca*, an Alfred Hitchcock movie. In 1942 during the Golden Apple Awards ceremony, he was awarded the "Sour Apple" award—meaning he had achieved the honor of being difficult to work with.

At age sixty-five, George Sanders ended his life because, as his suicide note revealed, he was "bored."

Not to sell Mr. Sanders short, he did obtain an Oscar and was nominated for a Golden Globe for his work on *All About Eve* (1950). He authored three books: *Crime on My Hands* (1944), *Stranger at Home* (1946), and his autobiography, *Memoirs of a Professional Cad* (1960).

Like Sean Connery, who told *Playboy Magazine* in 1965, "I don't think there is anything particularly wrong in hitting a woman," George Sanders once said, "A woman, a dog, and a walnut tree, the more you beat them, the better they be." Despite his obvious contempt for women, he did manage to marry four times. The most infamous were his unions with actress Zsa Zsa Gabor (1949-1954), then Zsa Zsa's sister, Magda Gabor, (1970-1971, just over a month).

Depending on the person who recalls George Sanders, he was either a great man of character and wit or a bitter and sullen human being. Maybe George let his most honest emotions out April 25, 1972, when he checked into a hotel in Spain, overdosed on Nembutal, and left a note that read, "Dear World, I am leaving because I am bored. I feel I have lived long enough. I am leaving you with your worries in this sweet cesspool. Good luck." He was sixty-five years old.

HERVÉ VILLCHAIZE

The majority of the public will remember Hervé as Tattoo on television's *Fantasy Island*. Fans of pop culture will squeal "De Plane! De Plane!" as fond memories of the pint-sized actor flood their Mountain Dew-soaked brains. For some, Hervé Villchaize will always be King Fausto of the Sixth Demension. It was his role in the cult classic film *Forbidden Zone* that shows he was an artist and an actor with a sense of humor. When funding began to dry up during the filming of *Forbidden Zone*, he donated his pay to see it completed. He had flair, and he had the ability to flaunt his flaws as well as his charm.

Hervé Villechaize was born April 23, 1943 in Paris, France. At a young age he stopped growing and was diagnosed with dwarfisim. This medical condition would later cause him great pain and play a large role in his death. Growing up, Hervé showed talent as a painter. At the age of twenty-three he moved from his homeland to New York where his expanding interest in art eventually grew into acting.

A man of such short stature is usually doomed to play roles of elves or time bandits. Not Hervé, he played a thug in *The Gang That Couldn't Shoot Straight* (1971) alongside a very young Robert De Niro. Hervé's voice was overdubbed since his accent was so thick. He also played a sheriff's deputy in *The Last Stop* (1972), a gay man who invites Jesus to dinner then makes a pass at him in *Greaser's Palace* (1972), a cannibal in *Malatesta's*

Growing up, Hervé showed

Carnival of Blood (1973), and most notably he played Nick Nack in the James Bond classic *The Man With the Golden Gun* (1974). Hervé played a wide breadth of roles. He was a man of short stature who didn't allow himself to be pigeonholed into sterotypical roles.

In 1978 Hervé landed the role that made him immortal, as the half-sized assistant to Ricardo Montalban on television's *Fantasy Island*. The show became a staple of primetime television, and Tattoo was the instantly recognizable ambassador. Feeling his character was integral to the show, Hervé demanded his salary be raised to match that of Ricardo Montalban. The producers balked at the request and decided it was easier to drop the character Tattoo from the show than to deal with or pay Hervé. In a 1991 interview with Howard Stern, Hervé stated he was still owed money from his work on *Fantasy Island* and had lawyers working on it.

Money wasn't the only problem the undersized actor faced. Hervé loved women, and wasn't always discreet with his emotions. He was said to have developed a fondness for Asian strippers while filming *The Man With the Golden Gun*. Then there is Mark Evanier, who has a very public dislike for Hervé. Evanier was a television producer who worked with Hervé on the show, *Rock 'n' Wrestling Saturday Spectacular* (1985). According to Evanier, ". . . instead of rehearsing and learning his lines, he spent his time ordering around male employees and discomforting female ones." How did Hervé discomfort the female employees? Evanier explains, "Because of his condition, Hervé had no strength in his hands. He could barely grip anything and certainly could not, he claimed, work his own zipper. Ergo, every time he had a costume change or a toilet break, he would stride

talent *as a painter.*

up to the most attractive woman around and insist she do the honors. And she would, in turn, complain to the producer, who was me."

With *Fantasy Island* behind him and a less-than-ideal reputation, Hervé began to work less. In the early '90s Hervé resorted to doing the one thing he strived to get away from. He appeared in a Dunkin' Donuts comercial, resurrecting his *Fantasy Island* catch phrase. Hervé shouts, "De Plain! De Plain! No! De Chocolate!" as the mustached Dunkin' Donuts worker scurries around to fill the order. In the interview with Howard Stern, Hervé said he was writing an autobiography. Not mentioned in the interview was that Hervé had found a companion named Kathy Self. Kathy was everything to Hervé in the final years of his life. She tried to help manage the pain Hervé felt as a result of his organs being too big for his diminutive size. She was his emotional support and his lover.

In the saddest part of this tale, not even the love or support Kathy Self provided Hervé could save him. He was taking more than twenty pills a day for his medical conditions. Because of his pain, Hervé often slept in a sitting position while leaning against a couch. He suffered from severe depression. Money was thin and work was unsteady, although he was in talks with The Cartoon Network to appear as Space Ghost's sidekick on *Space Ghost Coast to Coast*. The pain, the stress, and the emotions became too much for him.

On September 4, 1993, before the sun came up, Hervé wrote a note and took a tape recorder with him into his backyard. In the backyard he would hold two pillows against his body and fire a round from a handgun into his abdomen. Before firing the fatal round, he spoke into the recorder.

> "Kathy, I can't live like this anymore. I've always been a proud man and always wanted to make you proud of me. You know you made me feel like a giant, and that's how I want you to remember me." The note he left behind concluded with, "3am I can't miss with a dum dum bullet—Ha! Ha! Never one knew my pain. For 40 years or more. Have to do it outside less mess."

Kathy heard the sound of the gun firing and found Hervé outside bleeding. Despite her efforts to save Hervé by rushing him to the Medical Center of North Hollywood, Hervé succumbed to the injury.

Journalist Sacha Gervasi, who also has writing credits to the movie *The Terminal*, conducted the final interview Hervé gave before shooting himself. Gervasi sees Hervé's story as exceptional and needing to be told, "Hervé wasn't just a pop culture icon; he was one of the most charming, cultured, and dangerous people I've ever met. His is the story of a unique misfit trying to find his place in the world." Gervasi is currently in preproduction on *My Dinner with Hervé*, a biopic on the life of Hervé Villechaize. Viva Hervé!

CLARA BLANDICK

Born June 4, 1880 Clara Blandick began her career, like many others, acting on the stage. In fact she had an established career in live theater and no trouble landing roles in Hollywood. But it was one movie, one character, she would attach her name to that would make her a legend in movie history. In 1939 she played the role of Auntie Em in *The Wizard of Oz*.

It would not be the first or last time Clara would play the role of someone's aunt. Before retiring in the early 1950s, she was cast as an aunt at least eighteen times. However, by the time she retired, she had no loving family of her own. No immediate family anyway. Clara had married Harry Elliot in 1905 but they divorced in 1912. She had no children and was living alone.

In the twilight of her life Clara was suffering intense pain from arthritis and was beginning to go blind. She was eighty-one years old and decided she'd had enough. On April 15, 1962 Clara Blandick returned home from church and prepared a room for her final curtain call. The stage was set, pictures and tokens from her life were placed around the room. She changed into a fresh gown, and before taking a lethal dose of sleeping pills and tying a plastic bag around her head, left a note reading, "I am now about to make the great adventure. I cannot endure this agonizing pain any longer. It is all over my body. Neither can I face the impending blindness. I pray the Lord my soul to take. Amen."

LUPE VELEZ

Van Gogh is remembered as the painter who cut his own ear off when rejected by love. Lupe Velez is remembered as the actress who died by the toilet (or head in the toilet) when rejected by love. In the case of Lupe Velez, death by toilet is an unconfirmed urban legend. The rumor gained momentum when Kenneth Anger wrote the book *Hollywood Babylon* in 1959. Andy Warhol depicted her suicide in his film *Lupe* in 1965, further promoting the tale. The truth is there is no hard evidence to support the rumor, and other reports have her body being discovered in her bed.

What's more horrifying than the actual death of Lupe Velez are the events that led to it. From an early age, Lupe was known as a child with a wild streak. Her parents sent her to a boarding school, but Lupe returned unreformed. In her late teens she left her home country of Mexico for Hollywood with hopes of becoming a star.

Lupe Velez married Johnny Weissmuller, who played Tarzan, but the marriage did not last.

The natural beauty soon found work and before long was getting steady work. She appeared alongside Douglas Fairbanks and Jimmy Durante. Hollywood had provided more than an acting career, it also provided Lupe with a husband. In 1933 Lupe Velez wed Johnny Weissmuller, the man who portrayed Tarzan in the movies. Like so many other tales of woe, their marriage dissolved after five years.

Troubled romance seemed to be a specialty for the young actress. Lupe was getting a bad reputation, as she was known to date her costars. Her relationship with Douglas Fairbanks failed and her bond with Gary Cooper was broken when he refused to marry her. The tattered remains of her love life were considered hot gossip and often rife with untruths. Eventually, outright lies of her being a prostitute before coming to America began to circulate.

The blow Lupe would never recover from came in the form of an actor named Harald Maresch. While dating, Lupe became pregnant with Harald's child. He refused to marry. She refused to have an abortion, which was illegal at the time. Racked with guilt and left alone to deal with an unwanted pregnancy, Lupe took the final exit on December 13, 1944. Like Clara Blandick, Lupe arranged the room with flowers, candles, and photos before changing into silk pajamas and taking a lethal dose of sleeping pills. The note she left behind read, "To Harald, May God forgive you and forgive me too, but I prefer to take my life away and our baby's before I bring him with shame or killing him, Lupe." She was thirty-six years old.

JONATHAN BRANDIS

April 13, 1976 was the day Jonathan Brandis was born. Before beginning his acting career in 1986, he had already spent roughly four years as a child model. Five years after his first television appearance, he made his way onto the big screen with a minor role in *Fatal Attraction*. In 1989 he was given a larger role in the eye-rolling thriller *Stepfather II* about a man who marries into family after family only to kill them. *Stepfather II* led to his first starring role in the unnecessary sequel, *The Neverending Story II: The Next Chapter*. There is no denying that many cheesy movies bear the name Jonathan Brandis. He managed to pull off being in movies with Rodney Dangerfield (*Ladybugs*) and Chuck Norris (*Sidekicks*) in the same year (1992). The universe was either

There is no denying that many cheesy movies bear the name Jonathan Brandis.

aligned perfectly or he lost a bet. No, he wasn't working with Federico Fellini, but he was living his dream.

Jonathan Brandis wasn't happy being just an actor. He performed charity work with Make a Wish Foundation, Pediatric AIDS, and the Spina Bifida Foundation. He told *Starlog* magazine in 1995, "As I see it, part of the whole reason for being a celebrity in the first place is to use that notoriety to give something back. Not just to play star and show up at every Planet Hollywood opening."

Knowing no one stays a heartthrob forever, Jonathan branched out into other areas of filmmaking and television. He wrote an episode of *seaQuest DSV* where he also played the character Lucas Wolenczak. In 2003 he directed and produced *The Slainesville Boys*, a short film about two brothers on opposing sides of the Civil War. He had talent. He had promise. He had the drive to succeed no matter what. Unfortunately, he was also troubled. On November 11, 2003, a friend found Jonathan in his apartment, where he had hung himself. Paramedics took him to Cedar Sinai Medical Center where he died the following day. Jonathan did not leave a note. No one knows the exact reason why he hung himself. Friends and family speculated the causes to be a drinking problem and artistic opportunities slowing down.

JUSTIN PIERCE

Justin Pierce was just another kid on a skateboard until his path crossed with controversial director Larry Clark, who is known for highly sexual scenes involving teenagers and mixing non-actors with trained actors in his movies. He discovered Justin skating the streets of New York and cast him into the infamous movie *Kids* (1995) as Casper, one of the out-of-control teens.

Justin was born in London, England, on March 21, 1975. The Pierce family moved from London to the Bronx while Justin was still a small child. Those who knew him say he had a harsh childhood. Marianne Hagan, who costarred with Pierce in the 1991 independent film *Pigeonholed* recalled, "He had this expressive face that you don't have if you've had a happy-go-lucky life, and he wore it like a badge of honor."

As a teen Pierce picked up skateboarding and took to the culture associated with it. While many adults find skateboarding of-

One particular rumor said he connected with a crystal meth dealer and would disappear for days.

fensive or even unlawful, Pierce saw it as an outlet. Surprisingly, it became an outlet that would offer him the opportunity of a lifetime when he met Larry Clark. After *Kids* Justin decided to take a stab at acting full time. Soon he was landing small roles:*A Brother's Kiss* (1997), a supporting role in an HBO movie, *First*

Time Felon (1997), work in independents like *Pigeonholed* (1999), and even alongside Ice Cube in *Next Friday* (2000).

From the outside, his personal life appeared to be as promising as his professional one. He married in 1999 to his girlfriend, Gina Rizzo. He had good friends and two dogs he loved. There is no completely accurate answer as to what went wrong. Rumors were circulating Justin had a drug problem. One particular rumor said he connected with a crystal meth dealer and would disappear for days.

In early July of 2000, Justin Pierce checked into The Bellagio Hotel in Las Vegas. On July 10 his body was discovered by hotel security. The twenty-five-year-old actor had hung himself, leaving two suicide notes behind. The contents of the notes were never disclosed, leaving many to wonder exactly what went wrong. Was he distraught over his career? Did he never get over his rough childhood? Was he overcome by an addiction to drugs?

After his death two memorials were held for Justin in Manhattan: one at a Catholic church and the other outside a skate shop where he was a regular. At the time of his death, Justin was still working on a movie called, *Looking for Leonard*. Due to his death and budget issues, *Looking for Leonard* was not released until 2002.

DE'ANGELO WILSON

De'Angelo Wilson never had a chance to become a household name. With only two acting television roles (one of them a pilot that never aired) and four movie roles, De'Angelo would put an end to his life before he turned thirty. De'Angelo is most remembered as DJ Iz in the Eminem self-congratulating rap semi-biopic *8Mile*.

De'Angelo was born in Dayton, Ohio, on March 29, 1979. Life growing up wasn't always easy, and De'Angelo was no stranger to the foster care program. He dropped out of high school, opting to earn his GED instead. Despite the problems he experienced, he was determined to make a better life for himself. De'Angelo enrolled at Kent State University, where he honed his skills as a theater major and was well liked by classmates.

While still a student, De'Angelo suddenly seemed to be on the fast track to fame. He was cast in the prominent role as DJ Iz in *8 Mile* (2002); then shortly after that, he was cast as young Jesse in the Denzel Washington-directed *Antwone Fisher* (2002). Then the roles stopped, as if someone had thrown a rod in his spokes. In 2004 he appeared in one episode of *CSI: NY*. After *The Salon* (2005) was released, De'Angelo did work on one last film, *Mercy Street* in 2006. However, aside from a trailer still visible on the Internet, little is known about the movie.

De'Angelo wasn't just a DJ in the movies; he was one in his personal life as well. The real-life Antwone Fischer recalled, "He was such a fun and funny guy. I'd have backyard parties, and

"He was such a fun and funny guy."

De'Angelo would always come an hour early to help me set up. He'd tell great jokes . . . It's just real hard to think of a guy that happy and fun getting down so low."

But De'Angelo did get down so low. On November 26, 2008, his body was found hanging in the back room of a commercial building. It took authorities a week to locate his next of kin. De'Angelo had reestablished a relationship with his birth mother, Debra Wilson, and she had talked to him six weeks before his death. She told the media, "He got depressed. His career kind of failed, and I think he was beating himself up. Things were real down, and he just didn't know how to pick himself up." Wilson was unable to afford to bring his body home. De'Angelo's friends rallied together, raising the money to send their companion and colleague back to Dayton one last time.

SWAN SONGS: CELEBRITY SUICIDES

BARRY BROWN

The story of Barry Brown is beyond depressing. Donald Barry Brown was born on April 15, 1951 in San Jose, California, into a family with addiction issues. While he was still a small child, his mother was arrested for arson and second-degree murder. The charges were eventually dropped when the only witness wasn't considered credible. However, she was later sent to prison for tax evasion.

His face began to bloat and

Barry Brown (right) with his costar Jeff Bridges (left) from the 1972 classic Bad Company.

Barry received a letter from his brother, James, **begging him** *to sober up.*

164

While his mother was in prison, Barry immersed himself in books. By age eleven he had already skipped two grades. A constant overachiever, his IQ was 170. He could speak French and Spanish. It would be hard to find a child with the intelligence and potential Barry possessed.

Growing up wasn't always easy in the Brown family. Fighting wasn't uncommon when the mother returned home, having served her time. Divorce soon followed, after their father's affair with the babysitter came to light. The members of the Brown

he sweated profusely.

family sought solace in their own ways. Some chose seclusion, most seemed to self-medicate, but while young Barry did participate in some self-destructive indulgences, he also found escape in the movies.

Barry became a child actor, appearing in local plays and making his big-screen debut (although uncredited) at age seven in *All's Fair in Love and War* (1958). Entering his twenties, Barry began finding more high-profile work, appearing in numerous television shows like *Gunsmoke*, *The Mod Squad*, and *Night Gallery*. But the big break came in 1972 when he landed a role opposite Jeff Bridges in the western classic *Bad Company*. The tale of two young men dodging the draft in 1863 (before draft-dodging was cool) deserves as much respect as anything Clint (the snarl) Eastwood was in.

After *Bad Company* Barry appeared in a string of films that were poorly received by critics, and he found himself back in the world of television. At this point, Barry's drinking was out of control. His face began to bloat and he sweated profusely. In 1978 Barry played the role of a nameless trooper in what would be his final film. *Piranha* was a B horror movie produced by horror icon Roger Corman and directed by a young Joe Dante, who later made the classic horror/comedy/holiday flick *Gremlins*.

Piranha is a wonderfully cheap knockoff of *Jaws* with plenty of anti-war sentiment thrown in for good measure. Barry played a trooper who arrests the heroes of the movie and unknowingly puts a roadblock in their way of saving humanity. It's sad to see this young man's talent cut down to a few lines for a no-name character.

Piranha was the first film work Barry had done in three years. Director Joe Dante remembered Barry as a good friend who loved movies and wrote for horror movie magazines. It's hard to imagine that the actor who once had a promising career would be content ending it by working with Roger Corman.

In June of 1978 Barry received a letter from his brother, James, begging him to sober up. Both of the brothers were struggling with addiction, but Barry's appeared to be more out of control. The brothers made plans to dry out together and be the support the other needed. James was to pick up Barry on a Friday afternoon after he finished finals for his college semester. Friday came for only one of the brothers. James received a call from his stepmother notifying him that Barry had shot himself on Tuesday, June 27, 1978.

Sometimes it is hard to understand why someone would take the final exit. In the book *The Los Angeles Diaries* written by Barry's brother, James Brown, he reflects, "'All work,' my father used to tell us, 'is noble. Especially work that pays well.' And I wonder if this is why I find myself in Hollywood again, because I don't make enough writing novels, if it's just about money, if it's that simple. I wonder, too, if my brother saw it this way, and if, at any point in his brief life, he considered it something of a mistake."

Tragedy visited the Brown family again in 1997 when sister, Marilyn Brown, jumped to her death from a Los Angeles overpass.

CAROLE LANDIS

In 1944 Carole Landis attempted to commit suicide. In 1946 Carole Landis attempted to commit suicide. In 1948 Carole Landis committed suicide. The pretty ones are always troubled. That last statement is neither fair nor accurate as Carole was not a pretty woman. She was downright beautiful.

When Carole Landis was born, her father had already abandoned her mother and the family. By the time she was four, her mother had remarried, and the man she had known as her father

Carole Landis in the studio of Armed Forces Radio

abandoned the family. Nothing short of a sad beginning in the life of a woman who wanted to share her love and talent with the world.

As a teen, Landis (her real name was Frances Ridste) had no intentions of seeking out a normal life. By sixteen she had dropped out of high school and moved to San Francisco to begin her career as an entertainer. Her earliest jobs included dancing in a Hawaiian-themed night club and singing in several others. By eighteen she landed her first Hollywood contract and received regular work. Gossip was rife about how a newcomer was able to climb the ladder so fast. It was no secret Landis obtained her earliest acting roles along with her contract in exchange for sex. The infamous casting couch.

During her short life and even shorter career, she starred in over fifty movies. The exact number of films she appeared in is

The pretty ones are

unknown as her early parts were minor and often uncredited. She was married five times and had numerous relationships with men. Though it never stopped her from trying, she was never able to fill the void left by her fathers. She was an independent soul but not always by choice.

Carole Landis knew what she wanted and wasn't afraid to do whatever was necessary to get it. Even if what was necessary was also scandalous. The early tabloid papers loved her maybe even more than she loved herself. At twenty-nine years old, Carole Landis had burned her candle at both ends. And even though that candle had yet to reach its middle, she had had enough and blew the flames out herself.

On July 5, 1948, Carole Landis overdosed on barbiturates. Her professional career was fading. Her personal life was a mess of rejected love. The suicide note she left for her mother reflects the pain and inner turmoil she felt. It read—

> "Dearest Mommie—I'm sorry, really sorry, to put you through this but there is no way to avoid it. I love you, darling. You have been the most wonderful mom ever and that applies to all our family. I love each and every one of them dearly. Everything goes to you. Look in the files and there is a will which decrees everything. Good bye, my angel. Pray for me—Your Baby."

always *troubled.*

14

We're Gonna Need a Bigger Casket

FAME DOESN'T ALWAYS GO TO SOMEONE'S
head. Sometimes it goes to their stomach. The
glut of fame and fortune allows people to experience things previously unavailable—good food,
servants to clean up after them, more good food,
expensive booze, and maybe one of those fan-
tastic massage chairs. Getting fat and lazy can
happen to the best of us, but when you've got
the money, it's go big or go home. Just look at
Brando.

Here are a few of Hollywood's heavies whose heft may have lead to their deaths—

SHELLEY WINTERS

Died: January 14, 2006 (age 85)

Shelley Winters gave some memorable performances throughout her life. Some fans may site her role as Petronella Von Daan in 1959's *The Diary of Anne Frank* or as Charlotte Haze in 1962's *Lolita*. While others will always remember her role as the hysterical Belle Rosen opposite Jack Albertson and Ernest Brognine in 1972's *The Poseidon Adventure*. Shelley Winters was a rare being in that she was a movie star who didn't rely on good looks to get parts. As time went on, her weight and appearance were out of control. She went from curvy, or full figured, to medically obese. Critic Pauline Kael writing in *The New Yorker* about Winters's performance in Paul Mazursky's *Next Stop,*

Fat, morose, irrepressible, she's a force that would strike terror to anyone's heart

Greenwich Village (1976), said: "With her twinkly goo-goo eyes and flirty grin, [she's] a mother hippo charging—not at her son's enemies but at him. Fat, morose, irrepressible, she's a force that would strike terror to anyone's heart, yet in some abominable way she's likable."

JACKIE GLEASON

Died: June 24, 1987 (age 71)

The television show *The Honeymooners* (1955) made Jackie Gleason a household name. Later Gleason would show he could pull his weight in filmland. Some of the roles he played were Sherrif Buford T. Justice in *Smokey and the Bandit* (1977) and the comic villian Ulysses Simpson in *The Toy* (1982). His most bizarre role was the in the 1968 LSD-laced psychotronic flick *Skidoo*. Gleason plays tough Tony Banks, a mobster who smuggles himself into prison and takes orders from Groucho Marx

"To the MoonPie!" Jackie Gleason (right) with Brendan Behan (left)

who plays a mob boss named God. If that's not weird enough, Gleason's character has an acid trip that plays out on screen.

Nothing in Common (1986) with Tom Hanks would be Gleason's last role. He managed to finish filming the movie while fighting cancer. Weight problems were not helping his health, but the up-to-six packs of cigarettes a day was worse. He later died in his home. The mausoleum where he is buried bears the inscription, "And away we go."

LOU COSTELLO

Died: March 13, 1959 (age 52)

Bud Abbott without Lou Costello is like taking the chocolate out of peanut butter cups. The average person these days may not recognize one of the names alone, but when you put the two together—Abbott and Costello—they'll probably have an aha moment as they recall the comedy routine, "Who's on first?" Lou Costello was always a big man. It was a part of who he was, who his character was, and part of his comedic persona. You grow to love the character as a fat guy and soon couldn't imagine him any other way. Take note of that, Seth Rogen.

Abbott and Costello built a comedy empire. Their 1948 *Abbott and Costello Meet Frankenstein* is a pairing of horror and comedy that predates *Shaun of the Dead* by fifty-six years. As fate would have it *The 30 Foot Bride of Candy Rock* would be the last film for Lou Costello, and it would be without his comedy partner. The large actor died of a heart attack shortly after completing the film. Supposedly, his last words were, "That was the best ice-cream soda I ever tasted."

ORSON WELLES

Died: October 10, 1985 (age 70)

Orson Welles is a Hollywood legend. He created what is largely considered the best movie ever made, *Citizen Kane*

(1941). Ironically, the "best movie ever made" also caused Welles numerous problems in his professional career due to the main character being based on real-life newspaper tycoon, William Randolf Hearst. To put it in modern-day terms Orson Wells was the first person to make a movie taking on Fox News. Hearst was wealthy, powerful, and had numerous connections in the entertainment industry.

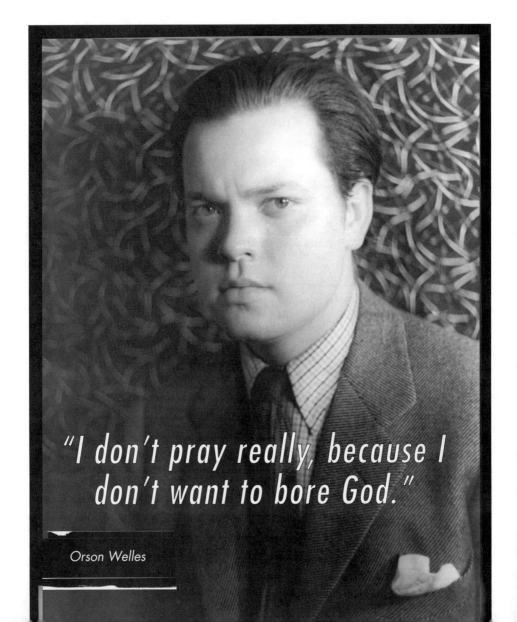

"I don't pray really, because I don't want to bore God."

Orson Welles

Welles would self-finanace another movie, *The Other Side of the Wind,* which was unfortunatly never completed. In 1973 he played Long John Silver in an adaptation of *Treasure Island.* In 1986 he provided the voice of Unicron, a planet-eating robot in *The Transformers: The Movie.* He also made television commercials. Outtakes of these commercials exist that show Welles three sheets to the wind and unable to recite his lines.

The writer, director, and star of *Citizen Kane* died two hours after being interviewed on the *Merv Griffin Show.* He weighed almost four hundred pounds at his time of death. He once said in an interview, "I don't pray really, because I don't want to bore God."

MARLON BRANDO

Died: July 1, 2004 (age 80)

Compare Marlon Brando in *A Streetcar Named Desire* (1951) to Marlon Brando in his last film, *The Score* (2001), and you'll probably ask yourself, "What the hell happened?" The man was an acting powerhouse. He was in one of the greatest mafia movies ever made, *The Godfather* (1972). As he became an established actor and eased his way into being a superstar, he became known as a demanding figure on set. Brando knew what he wanted. Everyone else could go to hell. His arguments with director Frank Oz on the set of *The Score* were legendary. The rotund actor was said to not take direction from Oz unless they were in separate rooms. Brando was said to refer to Oz as "Miss Piggy" in reference to Oz's work on *The Muppet Show.*

Over the years, the eccentric Brando's weight swelled to over three hundred pounds. His weight caused his health to decline, and he suffered from diabetes. When he died, a lawyer for the Brando family stated that the cause of death would be withheld for privacy concerns.

JOHN CANDY

Died: March 4, 1994 (age 43)

John Candy, another actor whose weight might as well have been his signature, always seemed to be smiling. He always seemed like a good guy. He appeared in the comedies *The Great Outdoors* (1988), *Uncle Buck* (1989), and *Nothing But Trouble* (1991).

"Rest in peace, make God laugh."

While working on *Wagons East* (1994), John Candy died from a massive heart attack in his sleep. Heeding the warnings from doctors, he had been making a conscious effort to lose weight and had even stopped smoking. His death left a hole larger than life in the world of film and comedy. After his death, the sign at the Laugh Factory comedy club read, "Rest in peace, make God laugh."

CHRIS PENN

Died: January 24, 2006 (age 40)

On January 23, 2006, *The Darwin Awards,* featuring Chris Penn, premiered at the Sundance Film Festival. The next day Chris Penn died, not from drugs as many suspected, but from heart disease. Chris Penn had an acting career with a wide range—from *Rumble Fish* to *Footloose* to *Reservoir Dogs*. He made his own name as an actor instead of riding on the coattails of his brother, Sean Penn. He was known to use numerous drugs, which did not contribute favorably to his health.

Sean Penn would later appear on *Larry King Live* and comment, "It was a natural death. But a natural death that was brought on by some hard living, but particularly weight."

VICTOR BUONO

Died: January 1, 1982 (age 43)

Victor Buono had a varied career, playing a priest in *The Greatest Story Ever Told* and King Tut on the 1960s *Batman* television series. He was nominated for an Oscar for his role as Edwin Flagg in *What Ever Happened to Baby Jane?* On top of his successful acting career, Buono put out a comedy album entitled "Heavy!" He was known for his king-sized appetite and making people laugh. He died in his home from a massive heart attack.

WILLIAM FRAWLEY

Died: March 3, 1966 (age 79)

Best known for his role as the robust Fred Mertz on *I Love Lucy*, William Frawley worked in vaudeville and then film before appearing on the small screen. He was considered a misanthrope and an alcoholic, who was impossible to work with. Frawley and his *I Love Lucy* costar, Vivian Vance, were offered a spin-off at the end of *Lucy*'s run. Vance despised Frawley so much she refused to do it. Frawley died from a massive heart attack while walking down Hollywood Boulevard. As a symbol of friendship, Desi Arnaz purchased a full page in the trade papers: In the space was a picture of Frawley and the caption "Buenas noches, amigo."

WILLIAM CONRAD

Died: February 11, 1994 (age 73)

William Conrad started acting on the radio before appearing in movies and television. He played Marshal Matt Dillon on radio's *Gunsmoke*, but when it crossed over from radio to television, Conrad was not given a role due to his weight. After a successful run in the entertainment industry, Conrad died from congestive heart failure. His girth originally affected his job opportunities and eventually led to his health.

15

Artists Who Had "Cut" Called Too Soon

Tyrone Power

BRANDON LEE

Born: February 1, 1965
Died: March 31, 1993

The son of the most famous Kung Fu star to ever make movies (Bruce Lee), Brandon Lee wanted to follow in his father's footsteps. Little did he know how much of his life would reflect his father's. Brandon made it into the movies, and in 1993 was filming the supernatural action picture *The Crow*. Unfortunately, like his father, Brandon would die making movies.

On March 31, 1993 the day's shooting was falling behind. In an attempt to catch up, the crew rushed making "dummy" bullets by pulling the tips off of real bullets, removing the gunpowder, and then reattaching the tip. While filming the scene, one of the tips became loose and lodged itself into the barrel of the gun. Later, for another scene, the same gun was loaded with "low power" blanks. When the blank was fired it provided enough force to propel the tip out of the barrel and into the torso of Brandon Lee. Paramedics were called, and the twenty-eight-year-old action star was rushed to the hospital for emergency surgery. The attempt to save his life was not successful, and Brandon Lee followed his father into the afterworld.

TYRONE POWER

Born: May 5, 1914
Died: November 15, 1958

Like many of his colleagues in the 1930s, Tyrone Power was born in a town that was much too small for him. He had aspirations of becoming an actor and set out to do just that. Starting on the stage, Power made his way to Hollywood where he made movies throughout the '30s, '40s, and '50s. Tyrone Power was often cast in adventure movies—a swashbuckling Romeo who could sweep any woman off her feet.

Living up to his name as someone who could keep going and

going, Tyrone Power continued to make movies with vigorous action scenes well into his forties. In 1958, at forty-four years old, he was filming *Solomon and Sheba*. He suffered a massive heart attack in the middle of a dueling scene and died. Like Clark Gable, Tyrone Power left behind a pregnant wife who gave birth months after his death.

KINJI FUKASAKU

Born: July 3, 1930
Died: January 12, 2003

Kinji Fukasaku was a man who wore many hats in the Japanese film industry. He was an actor, a writer, and a director. He is best known for the movies he made later in life—particularly

The only way to survive the attack was to climb behind or under other children, dead or alive.

two movies, *Battle Royale* (2000) and *Battle Royale II: Requiem* (2003). The *Battle Royale* movies (also known as *BR*) are ultra violent, and they place children at the forefront of the violence. The plot of *Battle Royale* revolves around a class of children who think they are going on a field trip but have really been selected, via lottery, into a type of reality game show where the students must kill each other off until only one is left. The survivor is the winner, and if more than one child is still alive after three days, they all die by having detonating explosives attached to their necks by a collar.

If this scenario sounds too far removed from reality, consider director Kinji Fukasaku was drafted at fifteen years old to deliver munitions during World War II. During the war Fukasaku, along with other children his age, were caught in a crossfire. The only way to survive the attack was to climb behind or under other children, dead or alive. After the attack Fukasaku had to bury children his own age. So, the story of *Battle Royale* could reflect the emotions of a child forced to fight in a war.

Kinji Fukasaku was already in the late stages of prostate cancer when *Battle Royale II: Requiem* went into production. Preparations were made for his son, Kenta Fukasaku, to take over directing duties in the event of his death. Kinji managed to direct one scene before succumbing to his illness. *Battle Royale II: Requiem* was released, and it was even more violent than the original. It's like *Saving Private Ryan* cast with children.

SERGEI BODROV JR.

Born: December 27, 1971

Died: September 20, 2002

If dying before a film was completed were a competition, Sergei Bodrov Jr. would win. He would win so completely that the other dead actors, directors, writers, caterers, or whatever wouldn't bother dragging their dead asses to the awards ceremony once they heard Sergei was in the running.

Sergei Bodrov Jr. was the son of a Russian playwright. Like father like son, Sergei Jr. had an artistic streak and began appearing in movies at the age of eighteen. From 1989 to 2002 Sergei appeared in eleven movies. He had won three awards for his acting and five awards for his first film, *Syostry* (2001). In the midst of all this work he married a woman he was madly in love with; he starred in a movie directed by his father, *Bear's Kiss* (2002); and fathered two children.

Life was good for Sergei, and in the second part of 2002 he set out to make his second movie, *The Messenger*. The movie was written by, would star, and would be directed by Sergei Bodrov Jr. Truly a crowning achievement for an artist his age. On September 20, 2002, Sergei and his crew were filming in the mountains of North Ossetia, a republic of Russia. Lighting conditions became poor around seven in the evening, bringing shooting to a stop. Then the unthinkable happened. The crew had been gathering equipment when a mudslide came rushing down the mountain in their direction. The mass of land and ice killed all who were on set. During the rescue attempt, only seventeen bodies were located. The rest, including Sergei Bodrov Jr., are still missing.

It's unfortunate when someone is killed on a movie set. An entire cast being wiped out at once is simply unheard of.

OLIVER REED

Born: February 13, 1938
Died: May 2, 1999

You always hope that when your time comes you'll die doing something you love. Oliver Reed couldn't have planned his own exit better if he knew it was coming.

Reed set off to become an actor after he served in the British army. His early work included acting for Hammer Studios, a much loved outfit known for cranking out cult classics. But Reed

He once vomited on Steve McQueen.

was able to show his skills in a variety of roles, including Frank Hobbs, the lover of the title character's mother in The Who's *Tommy* (1975). He played one of the Three Musketeers on three separate occasions. He also showed he could play dramatic roles, appearing in *Women in Love* (1969) as a man whose jealousy causes irreversible consequences.

Oliver Reed could also drink enough beer to fill a bathtub. In 1963 Reed landed himself in a vicious bar fight with an end result of thirty-six stitches in his face. In his face! He once vomited on Steve McQueen, the coolest man in cinema history, in the middle of a bender. His final night on earth included binge drinking and arm wrestling sailors. His exploits were jaw dropping. They could also stop people in awe as well as shock and disgust.

According to legend, his bar tab was well over $800.

On May 2, 1999, Reed was enjoying a break from the set of his latest movie, *Gladiator* (2000). While in a bar in Malta, Reed drank what could only be described as a heroic amount of alcohol. According to legend, his bar tab was well over $800. But all good things come to an end, and after a night of arm wrestling, rum, and drinking anything that wasn't paint thinner, Oliver Reed died of a massive heart attack. The bar was renamed to "Ollie's Last Pub" in his honor.

Meanwhile, back at the movie set, Oliver had not completed all his scenes before heading to that great drunk tank in the sky. Director Ridley Scott had some hard decisions to make, and in the end opted to spend three million dollars to digitally graft Reed's face onto another actor in post production. We could all only hope to be that big of a pain in the ass after we die.

HEATH LEDGER
Born: April 4, 1979
Died: January 22, 2008
The Australian actor may have been initially hired for his good looks, appearing in teen tripe like *Ten Things I Hate About You* in 1999. But Heath Ledger would prove his ability as an actor, gaining better and more challenging roles as his career moved forward. Ledger may have had some embarrassing marks on his

resume, such as the 2001 travesty *A Knight's Tale,* a movie that dared to combine the Middle Ages with rock music, but every actor eventually takes a part they're not proud of. He worked to show he had depth as an actor. The year 2005 was Heath Ledger's year, as he released three movies that raised his profile and placed him on the A-list. Ledger worked with visionary director Terry Gilliam on *The Brothers Grimm*; he played real-life California skater Skip Engblom in *Lords of Dogtown*; and then finally Ennis Del Mar in *Brokeback Mountain,* the movie that angered thousands of rednecks and grabbed the attention of countless others wanting to see Jake Gyllenhaal and Heath Ledger kiss. Not that *Brokeback Mountain* was pornographic, but there were women who saw these two hunks kiss and then understood why lesbian porn is so popular. *Brokeback Mountain* is a romance

"I couldn't stop thinking. My body was

story like many other countless love stories. This one happens to be about two men and is directed by Ang Lee, who, before then, was best known for the martial arts drama *Crouching Tiger, Hidden Dragon.* The movie was hugely successful, but had you told someone in 2003 that there would be a movie with Heath Ledger and Jake Gyllenhaal as cowboys madly in love with one another, *and* it's directed by the guy who made *Hulk*—no one would have believed it.

But it did happen, and *Brokeback Mountain* was one of the biggest and most-talked-about movies of the year. Ledger received a nomination for Best Actor in a Leading Role, Gyllenhaal received a nomination for Best Actor in a Supporting Role, and Ang Lee won the Academy Award for Best Director.

With his profile boosted, Ledger was able to be pickier about what jobs to take and obtain a larger paycheck at the same time.

When news broke that Ledger had been cast as the Joker in Christopher Nolan's highly anticipated Batman sequel, *The Dark Knight*, a number of fanboys went apeshit. Many were hoping to see an actor better known for their slanted persona, like Crispin Glover, snag the coveted role. Could Heath Ledger pull it off? Would he try to play it camp, or would he make the Joker a dark character? The naysayers worried that Ledger wasn't the right fit.

During post production on *The Dark Knight*, Heath Ledger was already working on his next project, *The Imaginarium of Doctor Parnassus*, his second film with director Terry Gilliam. Ledger was already doing interviews promoting *The Dark Knight*. He had nothing but confidence that the fans would love the movie. He said playing the Joker was "the most fun I've had playing a character."

exhausted, and my mind was still going."

The most telling interview Ledger gave was to Sarah Lyall and published November 4, 2007 in the *New York Times*. The interview reads like Ledger is having a panic attack in slow motion. Lyall describes Ledger as having "sleepy eyes" and dressed in "a hooded sweatshirt and ripped jeans hanging low" while he made coffee in his kitchen. In the interview Ledger says he's never really proud of his work. He fixates on the characters he played to the point of not being able to sleep. He'd take prescription medicines only to wake up an hour later. He told the reporter, "I couldn't stop thinking. My body was exhausted, and my mind was still going." Lyall went on to note that Ledger couldn't sit still, looking for things to fumble with or another cigarette to smoke. The interview makes it clear that Ledger is not comfortable—either not comfortable doing the interview or not comfortable in his own skin.

Only the people closest to him know if it was his dedication to work or something more that caused the actor to lose so much sleep. In an attempt to fight the insomnia, Ledger could be seen walking Washington Square Park just before dawn. He began to know others who frequented the park and played chess with some of them.

Ledger had made comments to the others on the cast and crew of *The Imaginarium of Doctor Parnassus* that he had not been feeling well and had trouble sleeping. Costar Christopher Plummer recalled nights of shooting in cold damp conditions. He felt Ledger had contracted walking pneumonia. On January 22, 2008, Ledger's masseuse was let into his apartment by security after he didn't answer the door for an appointed massage. His lifeless body lay in his bed. The masseuse dialed 911

That is an entire meal of pills.

and attempted CPR but it was too late. Ledger had died from what appeared to be an accidental overdose of prescription medicine. Not just a few sleeping pills though. The toxicology report showed Ledger died of "acute intoxication by the combined effects of oxycodone, hydrocodone, diazepam, temazepam, alprazolam, and doxylamine." That is an entire meal of pills.

The death of Heath Ledger was tragic. He left behind a young daughter, parents, and many friends. When *The Dark Knight* was released, critics and audiences agreed unanimously: Ledger's portrayal of the Joker stole the show. This wasn't just posthumous ass-kissing. The future of Ledger's unfinished movie with Terry Gilliam was uncertain. After some time it was announced that the magical element to plot would allow a different actor to finish the movie. In fact three different actors—Johnny

Depp, Jude Law, and Colin Farrell—would round out the final movie to feature Ledger. Heath Ledger will certainly be remembered as one of the people who left this earth before he showed his full potential.

16

More Mysterious and Ultimately Unresolved Celebrity Deaths

80 03

The grave stone of actress Elizabeth Short, whose body was found cut in half. She later became known as "The Black Dahlia."

BOB CRANE: Actor

Born: July 13, 1928
Died: June 29, 1978

Bob Crane managed to make it big as a disc jockey before striking into television and then the movies as an actor. In addition to starring on the television series *Hogan's Heroes*, Crane appeared in two Disney movies, *Superdad* (1973) and *Gus* (1976). Further into his career Crane's personal life begins to get real murky. Some say he was a sex addict, a theme the 2002 biographical drama *Auto Focus* runs with. On June 29, 1978 Crane was found beaten to death with a blunt object. It was later revealed semen was found on his body. The main suspect was John H. Carpenter (no, not that John Carpenter), a friend who had recently fallen out with Crane. The suspicions may have been high but the detectives couldn't prove their case. To date, the murder remains unsolved.

WILLIAM DESMOND TAYLOR: Director and Actor

Born: April 26, 1872
Died: February 1, 1922

William Desmond Taylor was born in Ireland, but left for New York City at the age of eighteen to pursue a career in acting. Taylor was able to find work as an actor but discovered his true calling was behind the camera. He directed over fifty movies and made a name for himself lobbying for a drug-free Hollywood. On February 1, 1922 Taylor was found dead in his home with a .38 caliber gunshot wound in his back. His wallet and cash were still in his pocket. His ring was still on his finger. Who could have done this and why? Over a dozen suspects were named.

In 1999 a witness claimed to have been with one of the suspects, an actress named Margaret Gibson, when she died in 1964. The witness claimed that just before she died, Gibson confessed to murdering William Desmond Taylor. One does have to question the validity of the testimony of a witness who waits thirty-five years to reveal a confession—especially when there is no way to confirm or discredit the claim. Officially, the case remains unsolved.

ELIZABETH SHORT: Actress

Born: July 29, 1924
Died: January 15, 1947

The most notorious unsolved Hollywood murder is that of Elizabeth Short. The murder has inspired books, television specials, and movies. It is a common belief that artists are more famous in death than in life—Elizabeth Short is one of those artists. She was a struggling, unknown actress, until her body was discovered in a vacant lot. She had been cut in two, right through her midsection. She was sliced from the corners of her mouth to her ears. Whoever killed the young actress knew what they were doing and took their time. The body was obviously posed, and her blood had been drained. The murder had taken skill—some might even say the skill of a doctor. The LAPD had a list of over one hundred suspects. Everyone who knew Short received a visit from the police for questioning. Over the years, dozens have confessed, many more have been under suspicion, but the murder remains unsolved. In death, Elizabeth Short obtained the nickname Black Dahlia.

MARILYN MONROE: Actress

Born: June 1, 1926
Died: August 5, 1962

While her latest movie, *Something's Got to Give,* was still in production, Marilyn Monroe's psychiatrist phoned police to say he had found the star dead. After an autopsy, her death was listed as a "probable suicide" from an overdose of barbiturates.

Despite the medical examiner's ruling, many believed her death was a result of foul play. Much of the gossip and rumor have the mafia or the Kennedy family delivering the lethal dose of drugs. So far, no one has been able to prove these speculations, leaving the official cause of death a probable suicide.

ALBERT DEKKER: Actor

Born: December 20, 1905
Died: May 5, 1968

Albert Dekker was the kind of actor who continued to work on both the studio lot and the stage after breaking into movies. His most notable role was in Sam Peckinpah's 1969 western, *The Wild Bunch*, playing Detective Pat Harrigan. Like a few others on this list, Dekker may have slid off into obscurity if he had not died in such a spectacular and vulgar manner.

On May 5, 1968 Dekker's fiancé, Geraldine Saunders, became worried when she had not seen or heard from Dekker in days. She convinced the building manager to allow her into his apartment and then fainted when they discovered the scene in his bathroom. Albert Dekker was naked, a noose around his neck, syringes in both arms; he was also gagged and handcuffed. Adding insult to injury, obscenities had been written all over his body in lipstick.

His death was ruled accidental, but the scene would lead others to speculate otherwise. If this were an accident, why was he handcuffed with syringes in both arms? The death appeared to be more like a murder committed by someone holding a very serious and personal grudge. Money and personal belongings were also reported missing from his home. That would mean he would've had to spend all of his cash and give away belongings before "accidentally" dying from autoerotic asphyxiation. And who doesn't do that?

The beautiful and sexy Marily Monroe was always a crowd pleaser. Although her death was ruled a "probable suicide," some believe there was foul play involved.

Movieland's Embarrassments, Failures, Feuds, Fights, Stalkers, and Prostitutes

17

Actors Who Started Off as Porn Stars . . . and Who May Have Gone Back to Being Porn Stars

ഇൗ ൙

MARILYN CHAMBERS
Porn—*Behind the Green Door* 1977
Pro—*Rabid* 1977

KAREN LANCAUME
Porn—*Anal Power 3* (1999)
Pro—*Baise-moi* (French for Kiss Me) (2000)

RON JEREMY
Porn—*What's Butt Got to Do With It?* (1993)
Pro—*The Boondock Saints* (1999)

JENNA JAMESON
Porn—*Up and Cummers 10* (1994)
Pro—*Private Parts* (aka *Howard Stern's Private Parts*) (1997)

(above) Marilyn Chambers
(left) Ron Jeremy

KATIE MORGAN
Porn—*Federal Breast Inspectors* (2006)
Pro—*Zack and Miri Make a Porno* (2008)

ASIA CARRERA
Porn—*Butt Watch* (1994)
Pro—*The Big Lebowski* (1998)

SASHA GREY
Porn—*Face Invaders* (2009)
Pro—*The Girlfriend Experience* (2009)

TRACI LORDS
Porn—*Night of Loving Dangerously* (1984)
Pro—*Cry Baby* (1990)

GINGER LYNN ALLEN
Porn—*On Golden Blonde* (1984)
Pro—*The Devil's Rejects* (2005)

AURORA SNOW
Porn—*Small Sluts Nice Butts 6* (2006)
Pro—*Superbad* (2007)

And believe it or not—
SYLVESTER STALLONE
Porn—*Stud* (1970)
Pro—*Rocky* (1976)

(top) Asia Carrera (above) Sylvester Stallone (right) Jenna Jameson

18

Factual Errors

MOVIES ARE FULL OF FACTUAL ERRORS.
Some are minor, like getting the color of the
boosters of Apollo 13 wrong in *Apollo 13*
(1995). While others are major, like the many
points of Bruce Lee's life that were changed for
dramatic purposes in *Dragon: The Bruce Lee
Story* (1993). On the following pages are just a
few factual errors from the silver screen.

Doom (2005)

A space marine and a scientist discover the enemies they're fighting have an extra chromosome, making them "superhuman." However, having an extra chromosome indicates Down syndrome.

Panic Room (2002)

Jodie Foster has locked herself in the panic room. In an attempt to force her out, the intruders fill the room with propane. Foster ignites the fumes by the vent, causing the ceiling area to be covered in flames, before the gas has a chance to reach the floor. Problem is, propane is heavier than the air we breathe, so when she lit the vent, the gas would already be by her feet, setting her on fire.

Gladiator (2000)

Russell Crowe's (Maximus) son cries out "I soldati!" which is Italian for "The soldiers!" All of this would be fine if the Italian language existed during the time of the Roman Empire . . . and if everyone else weren't speaking English.

The Da Vinci Code (2006)

Ian McKellen's character picks up a cell phone and dials 911. Help won't come if you dial 911 in the UK. He should have dialed 999.

Alone in the Dark (2005)

Poor, dumb Tara Reid is supposed to be the smartest person in the room but can't manage to pronounce "Newfoundland." She's a more convincing Bunny Lebowski than a scientist.

Equilibrium (2002)

When the storm troopers find a stash of art including the

Mona Lisa, they scan the painting and find it authentic. The Mona Lisa in the film is a canvas painting whereas the original is painted on wood. The painting in the movie is also too large.

Chronicles of Riddick (2004)

If direct contact with sunlight would cause a person to burst into flames, the surrounding air would be deadly, regardless if you're hiding in the shadows or not. The air in the shadows might be slightly cooler, but at those temperatures a person would still cook.

Casablanca (1942)

When *Casablanca* is shown on a map, it is further north on the coastline than it should be. Nitpicking, sure—but we're talking about what's supposed to be one of the best movies of all time.

Ghost Ship (2002)

Pointing out errors in a movie like *Ghost Ship* might seem redundant but . . . here goes. The ghost ship in question is supposed to be an Italian vessel, but written Italian phrases and words seen on the ship are grammatically incorrect. It's a major motion picture. Get a fact-checker or something.

Pearl Harbor (2001)

There are numerous factual and historical errors throughout the movie. The studio's response to these inaccuracies was that *Pearl Harbor* was meant to be a love story not a historically accurate retelling of history.

Jaws: The Revenge (1987)

Never mind this is a movie about a shark that holds a grudge when sharks aren't even capable of holding one. In this installment of the *Jaws* franchise, everyone's favorite killer shark lunges from the water, roaring with anger, to strike fear into his foes' hearts. Problem is, sharks don't have vocal chords. So a roaring, revenge-seeking shark makes about as much sense as a shark penning an angry letter to his congressman.

19

Made for TV Movies That Would Never Be Made Today

ၖၣ ಌ

Dark Night of the Scarecrow (1981)

A mentally retarded man named Bubba is the main suspect in a crime committed against a young girl. The town folk opt for vigilante justice instead of letting the law decide Bubba's fate. A lynch mob is formed, and Bubba is shot dead while hiding in plain sight as a scarecrow. If the idea of rednecks, with names like Skeeter and Harless Hocker, killing a retarded person sounds like a good way to spend a Thursday evening, then hold on—there's more! Turns out Bubba was innocent, oops. Luckily Bubba returns from the dead, as a scarecrow, and one by one picks off the rednecks who wronged him. Once all the villains are dead, he offers a a flower to a little girl, who asks if he wants to play a game. Which is more disturbing—a mentally retarded murderer, or a little girl playing with a dead person dressed up as a scarecrow?

Killdozer (1974)

There's nothing offensive about *Killdozer* but the mere fact that this movie exists is proof of the damages caused by cheap street drugs. What is *Killdozer*? It's the bulldozer that kills people—duh! If you're looking for a ridiculous plot, look no further. A meteorite turns a normal bulldozer into . . . a killdozer, taking *Spencer for Hire*'s Robert Urich as its first victim. These tough and seasoned construction workers hurl harsh insults at one another like, "You're a sour ball." One character in particular spits out random lines, like asking if anyone would like to go swimming immediately after lamenting his friend's death. Seriously, the only reason anyone would watch *Killdozer* is to see a bulldozer run wild. And it does at a whopping fifteen miles an hour.

> BEST LINE: "Sorry, pain makes me snide."
>
> BEST OBSERVATION WHILE VIEWING: Does no one realize they can outrun this thing on foot?
>
> INFLUENCED BY: Possibly the original *Thing* (for the isolation aspect). Drugs?

Bad Ronald (1974)

Ronald is a gangly young teen with bushy hair and thick-rimmed glasses. His mother suffers from a serious illness and tells Ronald, "One day you'll be a famous doctor." For whatever reason, she's waiting for her teenaged son to become a doctor before being treated for her illness. Ronald's uber nerdiness and strange attachment to his mother is explained as the boy not having a father figure in his life.

The neighborhood children pick on Ronald and call him names. When a little girl tells Ronald he's strange, he loses control and accidentally kills her. Upon hearing the tragic news, Ronald's mother comes up with a brilliant plan—wall up a bathroom in their old Victorian home and have Ronald live in the walls like a rat. And in case the metaphor of living in the walls like a rat is lost on you, there are shots of Ronald gnawing and nibbling on food like a rat. He crawls around the floor like a rat. He also eats ice cream with his hands.

Eventually Ronald is on his own when his mother dies during surgery. If only Ronald hadn't killed that girl, had completed medical school in four weeks, and had cured his mother. Dabney Coleman moves into the house with his wife and three daughters. Ronald watches the family through peepholes and becomes more rat-like, growing extra layers of grime.

Ronald isn't really bad; he's just really stupid.

Bates Motel (1987)

What's worse than Gus Van Sant's remake of *Psycho*? The made for TV sequel *Bates Motel*, a 1987 made for television sequel to the *Psycho* series. It stars Bud Cort (*Harold and Maude*), Lori Petty (*Tank Girl*), and for good measure, Jason Bateman (*Extract*) as a brooding young man needing the love of an older woman.

Bates Motel *fails on so many levels.*

Bud Cort plays a mental patient, named Alex, who has inherited the Bates Motel after the death of Norman Bates. Alex was Norman's best friend . . . awww. Alex reluctantly reopens the hotel when the hospital deems him fit for society once again. Lori Petty plays Willie, a wisecracking and lovable woman who has been squatting in the hotel since it closed. With the help of Willie, Alex is able to reopen the Bates Motel where strange supernatural events begin to happen. None of them have anything to do with the *Psycho* mythos.

Bates Motel fails on so many levels. It's not scary. The movie attempts to throw in handfuls of humor. It's not funny. It's an unwatchable mess—boring on all fronts. Bud Cort acts like a Muppet on LSD. Lori Petty acts like . . . Lori Petty. They should both be made to eat the film this was shot on. There are movies that are so bad they're funny. *Bates Motel* is so bad it's bad.

Splash Too (1988)

In 1984 Tom Hanks swam off into the sunset with Daryl Hannah in *Splash*. In 1988 Disney made a television sequel called *Splash Too*. Wow a sequel to *Splash* . . .wow. The original cast of *Splash* was so excited none of them signed up for a second go-round. They probably decided to let some new faces share in the fun.

Madison the mermaid has been updated with magical powers. A twirl of her finger turns a stream into a portal where Allen can see how New York is doing without him. What Allen sees is the family business going in the toilet. Allen and his understanding mermaid wife swim away from their tropical island back to New York. Just as guns in action movies only run out of ammo when it's related to a plot point, the swim to New York only takes a few minutes.

In true Disney fashion, there is joke after joke about Madison being a fish out of water. And in true Disney form, they're not funny. While Allen tries to save the family business, Madison sets out to save Salty the dolphin, who is trapped in an aquarium, in some mysterious testing facility, which shares space with a restaurant. Someone wrote a script where an evil science lab shares a door with a seafood restaurant.

The typical conflict of "But we're from different worlds!" happens, and, of course, everything is resolved an hour later. The only thing remotely interesting is the occasional cameo from Barney Martin, who would play Jerry Seinfeld's father, Morty, on the television show *Seinfeld* a few years later.

20
Flop!

REMEMBER THAT TIME YOU LOST TWENTY dollars and felt like a total idiot? That's nothing compared to the amount of money lost by the studios who put out the following movies. The following totals are estimates. PS: Madonna is so talented she's on this list twice.

Madonna

208

Osmosis Jones (2001)
Cost: $75,000,000
Total Gross: $14,026,418

Sometimes Bill Murray takes a job because he loves the script and wants to be a part of the project. Sometimes he takes a role to pay the bills. Murray's heart was probably in his bank account on this one. The first red flag for *Osmosis Jones* was no one wanted to direct the live action sequences until Murray signed on.

The Adventures of Baron Munchausen (1988)
Cost: $46,630,000
Total Gross: $8,083,123

Director Terry Gilliam is a man who seems to be cursed when it comes to filmmaking. Look at the 2002 documentary *Lost in La Mancha*, which details the series of events, each worse than the last, that ended up derailing his *The Man Who Killed Don Quixote* dream. *The Adventures of Baron Munchausen* wasn't much better. His budget was slashed, and the studio demanded changes. Gilliam did his best to make his vision come to life . . . but the adventure never got out of the gate.

The Alamo (2004)
Cost: $95,000,000
Total Gross: $25,819,961

Remember the Alamo (movie)! Not many do.

Alex Rider: Operation Stormbreaker (2006)
Cost: $40,000,000
Total Gross: $23,937,870

Perhaps Alex should change careers from spy to meteorologist. He's already got a name and gimmick worked out.

Ali (2001)
Cost: $107,000,000
Total Gross: $87,713,825

Sure it's not the biggest loser on the list but the story of one of the greatest athletes ever, possibly the greatest living athlete, deserves better than what *Ali* had to deliver. A slow, plodding story and Will Smith being miscast as The Greatest sunk this ship.

Breakfast of Champions (1999)
Cost: $12,000,000
Total Gross: $178,278

Kurt Vonnegut has style and a great sense of humor. *Breakfast of Champions*, the movie, was a loose adaptation, at best, of his novel of the same name, but it did pick up on its sense of humor. Bruce Willis playing Dwayne Hoover was fun to watch. Vonnegut found it "painful to watch."

Mohammed Ali was "the greatest," but the movie about his life, starring Will Smith, was not.

Cutthroat Island (1995)
Cost: $92,000,000
Total Gross: $10,017,322

You could blame the production company behind *Cutthroat Island* folding as the problem. You could say what others have, that Gina Davis was a bad choice for a leading lady. But come on! It's *Cutthroat Island*! You've seen it . . . or haven't. And that's the problem.

Delgo (2008)
Cost: $40,000,000
Total Gross: $694,782

Delgo is an animated children's movie—and that used to be enough to grab a kid's attention. However, Pixar came along and raised the bar so high for children/family entertainment that an animated film really has to shine to be noticed. *Delgo* does not shine. It currently holds the record for lowest earnings on an opening weekend.

Heaven's Gate (1980)
Cost: $44,000,000
Total Gross: $3,484,331

Heaven's Gate is a disaster that has since become legend. The movie tanked so hard it almost put United Artists out of commission for good. The original cut was almost five-and-a-half hours long. Critics at the premier were brutal, and the film was trimmed down to two-and-a-half hours. With the film heavily edited, critics still called the film boring, but now it was boring and disjointed. Massive amounts of money were lost, and *Heaven's Gate* became an albatross hanging around the neck of director Michael Cimino's neck.

McHale's Navy (1997)
Cost: $31,190,000
Total Gross: $4,529,843

In 1962 a television show called *McHale's Navy* hit the airwaves. On April 18, 1997 a movie called *McHale's Navy* was released to scoop up and euthanize what was left of the television show's cult following. Casting Tom Arnold in a lead role is never a good idea. His previous movie, *The Stupids*, should have been a giant, red, blinking light: "No! No! What the hell are you thinking!" Not even the legions of diehard Bruce Campbell fans (of *Evil Dead* fame) bought tickets for this sinking ship. *McHale's Navy* is the kind of movie no one worked on, rather they collected a paycheck.

Nothing but Trouble (1991)
Cost: $40,000,000
Total Gross: $8,479,793

Starring Dan Akroyd, Chevy Chase, and John Candy, this movie should have been right up the alley of every teen boy. What it turned out to be was an unfunny, unwatchable train wreck.

The Postman (1997)
Cost: $80,000,000
Total Gross: $17,626,234

If proof is needed that Kevin Costner has a massive ego, consider that every time he directs, he's also the star of the movie. Nevertheless, Costner outdoes himself in *The Postman* when the movie concludes with an unveiling of a statue of . . . who else but Kevin Costner. It's not clear if he really thinks he's that much better than everyone else, or if it's the world's most expensive cry for help. Whatever it was, no one came out to see the movie.

Shanghai Surprise (1986)
Cost: $17,000,000
Total Gross: $2,315,683

Sean Penn and Madonna, the Wonder Twins of ego, shat out *Shanghai Surprise* during their four-year marriage in the 1980s. Trying to figure out what is more ridiculous, Sean Penn as an Indiana Jones character or Madonna as some kind of Doctor Quinn missionary, is a coin toss. Don't lose the coin though because the total gross this film earned couldn't take it.

Swept Away (2002)
Cost: $10,000,000
Total Gross: $598,645

Guy Ritchie, you owe us an explanation.

21

Great Artists Who Made Bad Decisions

ଏ୦ ଔ

A SHORT LIST OF ARTISTS WHO MADE A film of critical and/or financial success only to embarrass themselves later.

(below) Robert De Niro, (right) John Travolta, (inside far right) Steve Buscemi, (outside far right) Ben Kingsley

DON CHEADLE: Actor

Accomplishment: *Hotel Rwanda* (2004)—Touching movie of a heroic person
Embarrassment: *Hotel for Dogs* (2009)—A movie you wouldn't want to touch

JOHN TRAVOLTA: Actor

Accomplishment: *Pulp Fiction* (1994)—Rebirth of an actor
Embarrassment: *Battlefield Earth* (2000)—Birth of a moron

MICHAEL CIMINO: Writer/Director/Producer

Accomplishment: *The Deer Hunter* (1978)—A film with scenes of psychological torture
Embarrassment: *Heaven's Gate* (1980)—A film that is psychological torture

ROBERT DE NIRO: Actor

Accomplishment: *Raging Bull* (1980)—One of the greatest character studies on film
Embarrassment: *The Adventures of Rocky and Bullwinkle* (2000) —One of the greatest moose studies on film

STEVE BUSCEMI: Actor
Accomplishment: *Fargo* (1996)—Played a perfect desperate man
Embarrassment: *Con Air* (1997)—Must have been desperate, man

ORSON WELLS: Actor/Writer/Director
Accomplishment: *Citizen Kane* (1941)—Defined what moviemaking could be
Embarrassment: *The Transformers: The Movie* (1986)—Became a warning of what moviemaking could be

BEN KINGSLEY: Actor
Accomplishment: *Gandhi* (1982)—Won an Oscar
Embarrassment: *BloodRayne* (2005)—Must have lost a bet

D.W. GRIFFITH: Writer/Director/Producer/Actor
Accomplishment: *Birth of Nation* (1915)—Groundbreaking work in direction and cinematography
Embarrassment: *Birth of Nation* (1915)—He's also a racist

ELAINE MAY: Writer/Director/Actress
Accomplishment: *Heaven Can Wait* (1978)—Nominated for an Oscar
Embarrassment: *Ishtar* (1987)—Won a Razzie for worst director and caused a nine-year gap between writing jobs

BOB CLARK: Director/Writer/Producer
Accomplishment: *A Christmas Story* (1983)—One of the most beloved holiday movies ever
Embarrassment: *SuperBabies: Baby Geniuses 2* (2004)—Considered one of the worst movies ever made

22

The Most Glamorous Profession Meets the Oldest Profession

ೞ൚ಌ

SAM ROCKWELL

While promoting his role as Victor Mancini, a sex addict whose life is turned upside down in the movie *Choke*, Sam Rockwell revealed some past moments that inspired him. In an interview with Wenn.com dated August 24, 2008, Rockwell was quoted, "I've been to prostitutes and massage parlors and stuff. Back in the old days."

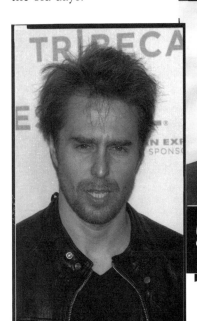

(left) Sam Rockwell (above) Charlie Sheen

ARTIE LANGE

Stand-up comedian, radio personality, and actor (mall Santa in *Elf*), Artie Lange has overcome a number of serious hurdles. His drug problems cost him his spot on *MADtv* and a stint in jail. Lange eventually got back on his feet and began appearing on the hugely popular Howard Stern radio show. Since working as a personality on *The Howard Stern Show*, Artie has learned to use his past problems as fodder for comedy. During a November, 2007 taping of *The Howard Stern Show*, Artie revealed he had contracted a STD from a prostitute at a bachelor party when he was in his twenties.

HUGH GRANT

On June 27, 1995, just weeks before the release of his latest romantic comedy, *Nine Months*, Hugh Grant was arrested for performing a lewd act in a public place. It was a lewd act with a known prostitute named Divine Brown. After being released from jail, Grant decided to keep his booked appearance on *The Tonight Show* with Jay Leno, where he told the host, "I did a bad thing."

CHARLIE SHEEN

In 2005 then-wife, Denise Richards, filed for divorce from husband Charlie Sheen. The marriage lasted four years and produced two children. The media went wild with speculation that Sheen must have wrecked his marriage due to his love of prostitutes. Sheen denies he went back to his ways, but at one point the man did spend $50,000 on Hollywood madam Heidi Fleiss's stable of high-end prostitutes. Charlie may have been a big spender with Fleiss, but, for whatever reason, she felt no love for her client, telling a journalist, "The guy's a rat." And "[Denise Richards should] take all the money and move on and forget about him." Perhaps Sheen wasn't a big tipper.

EDDIE MURPHY

On May 2, 1997, comedian Eddie Murphy picked up a transsexual prostitute named Atisone Kenneth Seiuli. Shortly after Seiuli entered Murphy's vehicle, they were pulled over by police. Seiuli claimed, "[Murphy asked] What type of sex do you like? I said I was into everything." Murphy claimed, "I was being a good Samaritan. It's not the first hooker I've helped out. I've seen hookers on corners, and I'll pull over, and they'll go, 'Oh, you're Eddie Murphy, oh my God,' and I'll empty my wallet out to help."

JACK NICHOLSON

Debra Winger costarred with Jack Nicholson in 1983's *Terms of Endearment*. In 2008 Winger published *Undiscovered*, an autobiography where she alleges Nicholson had a penchant for prostitutes. The smooth talker told her on a trip to Germany that "I should relax and enjoy the trip—and perhaps join him on his search for the perfect brothel." What really raised a few eyebrows was when Catherine Sheehan, a Los Angeles prostitute, filed charges against Nicholson. Sheehan claimed Nicholson refused to pay for sex, then became violent when she didn't leave. Nicholson wound up settling the case for $32,000. All work and no play, huh?

JODY GIBSON

Gibson, also known as "Babydol," released a tell-all book entitled *Secrets of a Hollywood Super Madam* in 2007. She claims her list of clients included actors Ben Affleck, Gary Busey (let's hope that girl got hazard pay), Jim Belushi, Bruce Willis, and movie producer Steven Roth. After getting busted by the cops, Gibson was convicted of running a prostitution ring and sent to prison for twenty-two months. While in prison Gibson was attacked, and her skull was fractured. One way or another, we all pay for love.

23

Marriages That Weren't Meant To Be

୫୦ ୬

NICOLAS CAGE AND LISA MARIE PRESLEY
The marriage lasted 107 days.

ZSA ZSA GABOR AND FELIPE DE ALBE
Married: April 13, 1983
Split: April 14, 1983 (Oh to be a fly on the wall that wedding night.)

RENEE ZELLWEGER AND KENNY CHESNEY
Filed for annulment after four months.

EDDIE MURPHY AND TRACEY EDMONDS
The marriage lasted just two weeks.
(Turns out the "marriage" wasn't legally recognized.)

BRITNEY SPEARS AND JASON ALEXANDER
Sure, she's primarily known as a singer, and it's not *that* Jason Alexander. But she did act in *Crossroads*, and the marriage to her "friend" lasted a little more than two days.

(left) Britney Spears (above)
Lisa Marie Presley (below)
Nicolas Cage

DENNIS HOPPER AND MICHELLE PHILLIPS

Eight days

ETHEL MERMAN AND ERNEST BORGNINE

Her fourth marriage, his third
Merman filed for divorce after thirty-two days of marriage.

DREW BARRYMORE AND JEREMY THOMAS

She was an actress, he was a bartender. It was the classic love story that lasted just over a month.

(below) Ethel Merman (right) Kenny Chesney (far right) Drew Barrymore

LIZA MINNELLI AND DAVID GEST

The wedding appeared to be an aging Polly Pocket play set on LSD. The marriage dissolved in less than a year and a half.

ROBERT EVANS AND CATHERINE OXENBERG

The marriage between the notorious producer and actress lasted a scant nine days.

24

Celebrities Who Made Sure Their Children Will Be Remembered

ᛞᛟ ᚲᚱ

Parents: **Gwyneth Paltrow** (actress *Iron Man*, *The Royal Tenenbaums* among others) **Chris Martin** (member of Coldplay along with cameos in *Shaun of the Dead* and television show *Extras*)
Children: **Moses** (son) born April 8, 2006
        Apple (daughter) born May 14, 2004

Parents: **Rachel Griffiths** (actress *The Rookie*, *Blow*, television series *Six Feet Under* among others) **Andrew Taylor** (production assistant on *SuperBabies: Baby Geniuses 2*)
Children: **Banjo** (son) born November 22, 2003

Parents: **Jason Lee** (actor *Mallrats*, *The Incredibles*, *Dreamcatcher* among others) **Beth Riesgraf** (actress *Scorcher*, *Alvin and the Chipmunks* among others)
Children: **Pilot Inspektor** (son) born September 28, 2003 (Lee was inspired by the song *He's Simple, He's Dumb, He's the Pilot* by indie rock band Grandaddy . . . that's gotta hurt)

Parents: **Penn Jillett** (magician and actor *Fear and Loathing in Las Vegas*, *Hackers* among others) Emily Zolten (not a celebrity but probably a very nice person)
Children: **Moxie CrimeFighter** (daughter) born June 3, 2005
(In a radio interview Jillett stated that his wife came up with the name CrimeFighter since people don't generally know each other's middle names.)

Parents: **Shannyn Sossamon** (actress *A Knight's Tale*, *One Missed Call*, *The Order* among others) Dallas Clayton (not a celebrity but clearly open to new ideas)
Children: **Audio Science** (son) born May 29, 2003
(That should rack up a hefty therapy bill.)

Parents: **Nicolas Cage** (actor *Raising Arizona*, *The Wicker Man* among others) **Alice Kim** (Cage's current wife)
Children: **Kal-El Coppola** (son) born October 3, 2005
(We get it, you like Superman . . . your kid might not.)

Parents: **Tom Cruise** (actor *Top Gun* among others) **Katie Holmes** (actress *The Gift* among others)
Children: **Suri** (daughter) born April 18, 2006
(Finally, a name that sounds like an IKEA product.)

Parents: **Nick Nolte** (actor *48 Hrs.*, *Cape Fear*, *Mother Night* among others, and one hell of a mug shot) Rebecca Linger (Nolte's third wife)
Children: **Brawley King** (son) born June 20, 1986
(This kid could kick your ass when he was five years old.)

(left) Gwyneth Paltrow has a daughter named Apple and a son named Moses.
(above) Katie Holmes named her daughter Suri—perhaps after an Ikea product.

Parents: **Robert Van Winkle** (aka Vanilla Ice, actor *Cool as Ice* . . . what else do you need?) Laura Van Winkle (wife)

Children: **Dusti Rain** (daughter) born sometime in 1998

        KeeLee Breeze (daughter) born sometime in 2000

(Future spelling bee champs. Now let's pack the bong!)

Parents: **Robert Rodriguez** (director *Sin City* and *El Mariachi* among others) **Elizabeth Avellan** (producer and vice president of Troublemaker Studios)

Children: **Rocket Valentino** (son) born September 14, 1995

        Racer Maximilliano (son) born April 16, 1997

        Rebel Antonio (son) born January, 1999

        Rogue Joaquin (daughter) sometime in 2004

        Rhiannon Elizabeth (daughter) August 12, 2005

(Whatever these kids do, let's hope they do it together because the names are pretty badass when you see them together)

Parents: **Spike Lee** (director *Do the Right Thing*, *25th Hour*, *Inside Man* among others) Tonya Lewis (wife and attorney)

Children: **Satchel** (daughter) December 2, 1994

25

When Your Biggest Fans
Turn Out To Be Crazy

&ℭ

STEVEN BURKY MEET JENNIFER GARNER

Steven Burky loves Jennifer Garner a little too much. According to Garner, Burky began stalking her in 2002. In her written statement, Garner stated Burky had been sending her "packages and letters containing delusional and paranoid thoughts and following me around the country." Burky went so far as to show up at her home, stating he had received a vision from God of Garner being persecuted, possibly resulting in her death. He was there to protect her.

The judge issued a three-year restraining order and later changed it to permanent. Burky is not to come within one hundred yards of Garner, her husband, Ben Affleck, or their daughter. He is currently under a 5150 hold in a psychiatric ward. Before being admitted into the hospital, he wrote a blog entitled "Satanic Panic."

ATHENA ROLANDO MEET BRAD PITT

Athena Rolando was only a teen when she became infatuated with actor Brad Pitt. Alas, he was older, and, at the time, taken by the beautiful Gwyneth Paltrow. So Rolando did what any teen girl would do—she began chanting to put a hex on the couple. In 2000 Rolando realized the chants weren't working, so she went to visit Pitt at his home. Figuring it worked for Goldie Locks, she climbed through a window and wandered around Pitt's home for ten hours, trying on his clothes and lying in his bed.

Athena was eventually discovered by a caretaker who called the police. Once under custody she was discovered to be carrying a book on witchcraft and a safety pin decorated with ribbons that she claimed was a doll. After her arrest, Rolando spoke to reporters saying, "I was going to give him the doll, and I was going to explain it to him and see what he thought." She ended with, "I hope he isn't angry with me."

> ... *she began chanting to put a hex on the couple.*

A restraining order was granted, and Rolando was sent to undergo psychiatric treatment.

DAWNETTE KNIGHT MEET MICHAEL DOUGLAS AND CATHERINE ZETA-JONES

Jokes were rampant when Catherine Zeta-Jones married Michael Douglas in 2000. Douglas was twenty-five years older than Zeta-Jones. Zeta-Jones was a sex symbol, Douglas showed his age. Dawnette Knight wasn't joking. She wanted Douglas for herself, and Zeta-Jones was standing in her way.

Knight began writing letters to Zeta-Jones, threatening to

cut her up in little pieces, "like Sharon Tate was," and feed to her dogs. During the trial Zeta-Jones took the stand, answering questions and reading aloud the letters Knight had written. In 2005 Knight was sentenced to three years in prison. She was found guilty of stalking and twenty-five counts of criminal threats.

DIANA NAPOLIS MEET STEVEN SPIELBERG

Diana Napolis, who formerly worked in child protection, believed there was a satanic conspiracy and those who did not acknowledge it were the ones raping and murdering children. The California woman was initially content with harassing school officials, memory experts, and a handful of other people.

Eventually Napolis spread her wings and began calling director Steven Spielberg, threatening to go public with a supposed

She claimed Spielberg had implanted a

satanic cult that met in the director's basement. She also claimed Spielberg had implanted a microchip in her brain called "soul catcher" that he used to control her thoughts and actions. Napolis did attempt to go public, she began handing out leaflets stating Spielberg had been, "monitoring a woman who had a devastating encounter with extraterrestrials." That woman was Diana Napolis.

In October of 2002 Spielberg was granted a restraining order, keeping Napolis at least 150 yards away from him. All this after a different stalker, named Jonathan Norman, planned to rape, yes rape, Speilberg in 1998.

DIANA NAPOLIS MEET JENNIFER LOVE HEWITT

On November 26, 2002, a little more than a month after Steven Spielberg was granted a restraining order, Diana Napolis was arrested for terrorizing Jennifer Love Hewitt. Napolis believed

Hewitt was part of the same satanic cult as Spielberg. Napolis began emailing death threats and attempted to confront Hewitt face to face by pretending to be a friend. Once arrested, Napolis admitted to getting in a shoving match with Jennifer Love Hewitt's mother. With her mom!

Napolis was committed to a psychiatric ward until she was found able to stand trial. On September 29, 2003 she pled guilty to stalking and was placed on five years probation.

On March 25, 2008 Napolis filed suit for ten-million dollars against a number of people, including a memory researcher and a newspaper publisher. Among her claims were, "victimization by nonlethal technology." It goes without saying—Miss Napolis is not a millionaire.

microchip in her brain called "soul catcher."

26

Why Can't We Be Friends?

ഓ ൙

SHANE BLACK VS. SONYA POPOVICH
Relationships Are Hard

Shane Black is known for his over-the-top action movies. His writing credits include *Lethal Weapon 1–4* and *Kiss Kiss Bang Bang*. Black has also been known for dabbling in acting. His most notable role was playing the foul-mouthed commando, Hawkins, in the 1987 sci-fi/horror flick *Predator*. Black's latest role is playing defendant as his ex-girlfriend, Sonya Popovich, takes him to court for five-million dollars. Popovich claims during their relationship Black was prone to lash out violently, often while high on drugs, and that Black beat Popovich so bad she had to be hospitalized. Then Black paid her a visit in the hospital where, according to Popovich's attorney, he, "crawled into [her] bed, removed a vial of cocaine from his pocket, sniffed some cocaine from the vial, and proceeded to masturbate in Plaintiff's hospital bed."

On March 27, 2009 Wenn.com reported Black was counter-suing Popovich. Black claims the allegations are false, and Popovich only filed suit when he refused to pay a 1.5 million dollar bribe.

QUENTIN TARANTINO VS. DON MURPHY
Take It Back!

When you mix an eccentric film buff famous for making gritty movies, not to mention criticized for his use of homage/plagiarism, with a producer who didn't enjoy working with said filmmaker, problems are bound to arise. Tarantino confronted Murphy in a West Hollywood restaurant in regards to unflattering comments Murphy made in an interview. It wasn't long before Don Murphy was on the receiving end of a fist. Tarantino later told *Variety*, "I really think I slapped some respect into the guy. We shook hands and agreed not to badmouth each other anymore." Murphy responded by filing a five-million dollar lawsuit for retribution. When asked about the incident, Murphy told *Entertainment Weekly*, "I didn't say I wished Quentin Tarantino was dead. I didn't say I wanted him dead. I just said I'd celebrate his death."

JOHN LOVITZ VS. ANDY DICK
When Words Fail You

John Lovitz has spent his career making people laugh. Andy Dick has spent his career confusing many and hurling himself into scandal. In 2007 Lovitz acted out on a long-held grudge

"I put the Phil Hartman hex on you. You're the next one to **die***."*

against Dick in a Hollywood comedy club. John Lovitz believed Andy Dick reintroduced cocaine to Brynn Hartman, the wife of comedian Phil Hartman, who had defeated substance abuse more than ten years earlier. It wasn't long after this encounter, Brynn murdered her husband then shot herself. Andy Dick, wanting to have the last word, told Lovitz in a restaurant, "I put the Phil Hartman hex on you. You're the next one to die." So when Dick appeared at comedy club The Laugh Factory while Lovitz was performing, it was the last straw. According to Lovitz, "I lost it and I grabbed him by the shirt and pushed him against the wall, and he's just smiling at me. I smashed his head into the back of the bar." Who knew John Lovitz could be a comedian and an action star?

BETTE DAVIS VS. JOAN CRAWFORD
What Ever Happened to Civility?

In her last book Bette Davis denied there was ever a feud between her and *What Ever Happened to Baby Jane?* costar Joan Crawford. Then again when American journalist Boze Hadleigh interviewed Davis for his book, *Bette Davis Speaks*, he asked if it was true that she once said, "There may be a heaven, but if Joan Crawford is there, I'm not going." Her reported response was, "Would you?" In the book *The Golden Girls of MGM*, Jane Ellen Wayne confirms the story of Bette referring to herself and Joan as "we two old broads" while promoting *What Ever Happened to Baby Jane?* which prompted Joan Crawford to, "(Send) her a note on her traditional blue stationary: 'Dear Miss Davis, Please do not refer to me as an old broad. Sincerely, Joan Crawford.'" Joan Crawford's husband was president of PepsiCo. She filled his empty seat on the board of directors after his death. Bette Davis had a Coca Cola machine installed onset just to mess with her. Tension became so thick that supposedly there wasn't much acting by the time the fight scenes were filmed.

JEREMY PIVEN VS. STEVEN DORFF
Rumble in the Boy's Room

Jeremy Piven was in *One Crazy Summer* (1986) and *PCU* (1994), so that's reason enough to take his side. Steven Dorff was in *FeardotCom* (2002), so for that alone he's in the wrong. The story goes that Piven stopped Dorff from trying to cut in line at New York's Bungalow 8 Club, calling him a "privileged, spoonfed, son of a bitch." Ouch! The two reportedly began shoving each other, and the name-calling went wild. Dorff, turning red, told Piven he made a huge mistake because he had powerful friends. Piven ended the encounter with, "You are done, see you in line for my next movie!" Time can heal all wounds, and two years later Dorff said the hatchet was buried. The fracas was a one-time encounter.

ROGER EBERT VS. VINCENT GALLO
War of the Words!

Roger Ebert is a movie critic with strong opinions on movies—with the knowledge to back them up. You won't always agree with the man, but he knows his material. Vincent Gallo is a filmmaker and a darling in the independent film circuit. Hipsters love him . . . Roger Ebert, not so much. The year was 2003, Gallo's latest film *The Brown Bunny* about . . . well, the movie's own plot description will tell you: "Professional motorcycle racer Bud Clay heads from New Hampshire to California to race again. Along the way he meets various needy women who provide him with the cure to his own loneliness, but only a certain woman from his past will truly satisfy him." Sound self-absorbed? Even more so when you find out the movie is written by, directed by, and stars Vincent Gallo. The movie is a dull buildup to see leading lady, Chloe Sevigny, blow Gallo on screen. Again, written by, directed by, and starring Vincent Gallo.

So Roger Ebert sees *The Brown Bunny* and promptly calls it the worst movie in the history of the Cannes Film Festival. Incensed by the review, Gallo launched back at the pudgy Ebert, calling him a "fat pig with the physique of a slave trader." But why stop there? Gallo also placed a hex on the critic, hoping he would get cancer. Proving to be the wittier of the two, Ebert shot back, "Although I am fat, one day I will be thin, but Mr. Gallo will still have been the director of *The Brown Bunny*." Again, why stop there? Ebert also acknowledged the hex, saying his last colonoscopy was more entertaining than Gallo's movie.

The two eventually called a truce, and Roger Ebert got thyroid cancer. Oops.

VAL KILMER VS. TOM CRUISE
Top Secret against Top Gun

In 1986 Kilmer and Cruise costarred in *Top Gun*, a movie about fighter pilots, egos, and Kelly McGillis doing stuff while "Take My Breath Away" plays. I don't know what started the fracas, but Tom's handsome rubbed up against and scuffed Val's rugged. What was reported was Val Kilmer and Tom Cruise disliked each other immensely and that dislike came to blows when Kilmer refused to appear at a charity volley ball game with Cruise. They took it to the danger zone.

VAL KILMER VS. THE ISLAND OF DOCTOR MOREAU
Can I Still Use You as a Reference?

Between *Top Gun* and working with director John Frankenheimer, Val Kilmer had built up a reputation for being extremely difficult to work with. He was an actor who was known to not break out of character and to throw tantrums when things did not go his way. *Buzz* magazine listed him as one of the "Twelve Scariest People in Hollywood."

"You are confusing your talent

In 1996 Val Kilmer was contractually obligated to film *The Island of Doctor Moreau*, a project he wanted no part of. Kilmer was also facing a public and nasty divorce from his wife. His attitude on set was poor, and a number of his coworkers were displeased. Trouble started early: In the first week of shooting director Richard Stanley was fired and replaced with John Frankenheimer. Kilmer and several of the actors often clashed. Marlon Brando was said to have snatched a cell phone from Kilmer and thrown it. Brando later told Kilmer, "Your problem is, you are confusing your talent with your paycheck." Another actor on the set, William Hootkins, referred to Mr. Kilmer as, "the worst specimen of humanity I've run across in a while. He's a monster." To drive the point home, when the final shot for Val Kilmer was over, director John Frankenheimer exclaimed, "Cut. Now get that bastard off my set."

CHRISTIAN BALE VS. THE CREW
A Fucking Amateur

If you've seen *American Psycho* (2000), *The Machinist* (2004), *Rescue Dawn* (2006), or *The Dark Knight* (2008), you know Christian Bale is serious business. The man is an acting machine who takes his body to dangerous levels to achieve his goal. He's also dead serious on set, as Shane Hulbrut found out on the set of *Terminator: Salvation* (2009). Shane Hulbrut was the director of photography who committed the unfortunate accident of stepping into Bale's line of sight while filming.

Bale later claimed the scene in question was intense and required great confrontation. Bale was upset on an epic scale and launched into a rant that lasted well over three minutes.

Bale: Hey, it's fucking distracting having somebody walking

with your paycheck."

up behind Bryce in the middle of the fucking scene? Give me a fucking answer! What don't you get about it?

Christian Bale

Shane Hurlbut: I was looking at the light.

Bale: Ohhhh, gooooood for you. And how was it? I hope it was fucking good, because it's useless now, isn't it?

Hurlbut: Okay.

Bale: Fuck sake man, you're amateur. McG (director), you got fucking something to say to this prick?

It goes on and on. Bale threatens to walk off the set if Hurlbut isn't fired, but in the end everyone kept their jobs and the movie was finished . . . with a PG-13 rating. Fart. Christian Bale later said he felt embarrassed by the rant and hoped his behavior wouldn't affect ticket sales.

DAVID O. RUSSELL VS. HUCKABEES
Where's the Love?

Artists by and large are eccentric people. Sometimes you need to put up with their idiosyncrasies in order to obtain truly inspired art. In the case of David O. Russell, you antagonize your artists to the point of physical confrontations. The man who wound up in a fistfight with George Clooney on the set of *Three Kings* (1999) caused mass mayhem on the set of *I Heart Huckabees* (2004). Reportedly Russell saw fellow director Christopher Nolan (*Memento, The Dark Knight*) at a social gathering and put him in a headlock, fearing Nolan may try to snatch one of his actors for a different project.

While on the set of *I Heart Huckabees,* Russell and actress Lily Tomlin fought so badly cameras were left rolling and the footage leaked to the Internet. In one confrontation Russell and Tomlin are discussing the physical movements for her to go through in the scene. Then Russell begins lashing out, "Fuck you! I'm just trying to help you!" He jumps to his feet, throwing everything off the prop desk Tomlin is sitting at, and exclaims, "Bitch!" He kicks a garbage can across the set calling Tomlin a "fucking cunt" as she stands there and takes it.

The next behind-the-scenes rant has Tomlin sitting in a car with Dustin Hoffman looking directly into the camera, giving the middle finger and yelling, "Fuck you, motherfucker!" at Russell. As her cast mates attempt to calm her down she fires back with, "Fuck you too." None of these actors look happy. They all look frustrated and confused. The tension must have been unbearable. Apparently at least one person needed help with their communication skills.

27

Alan Smithee: The Alias Men

EVERYONE HAS SEEN A MOVIE THAT THEY declare is the "worst movie ever made." But what happens when a director has made a movie that they feel has not lived up to their vision or even worse . . . have themselves created the worst movie ever made? From 1968 till the year 2000 there was a clause in the Directors Guild of America (DGA) that allowed directors to remove their names from a movie if they could prove they were not allowed control. Should the guild side with the director, the director's name was removed from the project and replaced with the pseudonym "Alan Smithee." The name Alan Smithee is an anagram for "The Alias Men." In return for no longer being affiliated with the movie, the director was not allowed to publicly discuss having been part of production or any connection to it.

Alan Smithee never went to film school. If he had it would have been correspondence classes offered on the back of gum wrappers. He's everywhere and nowhere. He's a ghost. Alan Smithee honed his art in making painfully bad movies. Shaming the film community was his pride. Alan Smithee died at the age of thirty-two when he rode the TriStar Pegasus off to Valhalla.

Some of Alan Smithee's film credits include:

Shrimp on the Barbie (1990) A romantic comedy where Cheech Marin plays a wisecracking, loveable waiter in Australia (wacky!) who is hired by a wealthy heiress to pose as her boyfriend to upset her father (wackier!). Guess when the laughs start? They don't. Cheech does his usual "Cheech" performance (minus the drugs) that just seems kind of sad outside of the Cheech

Alan Smithee is everywhere and nowhere. He's a ghost.

and Chong universe. Aside from that, *Shrimp on the Barbie* has the typical romantic comedy plot devices (see *Loverboy* or *Can't Buy Me Love*) but set in Australia to cash in on the Paul Hogan (*Crocodile Dundee*) craze.

Hellraiser Four: Bloodline (1996) After three movies about a box that opens the doors to hell. After three movies starring a villain who has nails sticking out of every other inch of his head. After people having skin stripped from their body, how could the franchise get scarier? Put it in space! And the villain, Pinhead, who had always been ominous, now kidnaps children and rattles on like a goth teen updating his diary.

An Alan Smithee Film: Burn Hollywood Burn (1998) What do you know, a movie poking fun at Hollywood and acknowledging the Directors Guild of America's ability to use the alias "Alan Smithee." And what do you know, it's so bad that the director had his name removed from the project and replaced with Alan Smithee. Is life imitating art or is art imitating life? The movie made back $45,779 of its $10,000,000 budget. When the Razzie awards (the anti-Oscar) came around *An Alan Smithee Film: Burn Hollywood Burn* picked up five awards including worst picture and worst screenplay.

28

Anna Nicole Smith: Grave Robber

IF A CRADLE ROBBER IS A PERSON WHO dates others who are much too young for them, then it would be safe to call Anna Nicole Smith a grave robber. It would be a lot more accurate to call her a grave robber than an actress. But the woman did appear in movies and she kinda remembered her lines and her marks . . . so for the sake of this book, we're calling her an "actress."

The story of Anna Nicole Smith is a very smutty rags-to-riches tale. Born Vickie Lynn Hogan in glamorous Harris County, Texas, on November 28, 1967, Anna Nicole grew up falling into many stereotypes of the area. Not being a learnin' type, she dropped out of high school sophomore year. She met and married her first husband at the age of seventeen while they were both working in a fried-chicken restaurant. Two years later they separated, but not before giving Anna Nicole a chance to spawn a son at the age of eighteen.

Our busty blonde heroine then set out to work other soul-sucking jobs at establishments like Walmart to make ends meet. In her early twenties, working a low-paying job, and with a small child to take care of, Anna Nicole entered the noble field of exotic dancing. She aspired to be a modern-day Lana Turner, waiting for that moment to be discovered. When not entertaining bachelor parties and middle-aged men who were either virgins or bored to death of boning their wives or simply couldn't get a date, she worked on her craft and took modeling lessons.

Determined that modeling would be her trade, Anna Nicole went to an open audition for *Playboy* magazine. It was more legitimate than stripping, and she was paid in check form as opposed to collecting dollar bills from her thong and off the floor. The audition was a success. With a mixture of blood, formaldehyde, and erectile-dysfunction medication coursing through his veins, Hugh Hefner reached down his hand and placed Anna Nicole on the cover of *Playboy*.

In 1993 Smith was announced Playmate of the Year, which launched her from being a naked nymph in a glossy soft-core spread to legitimate model. She showed her assets in a series of print ads for Guess Jeans. *New York* magazine decided to take the piss out of Smith and published an article entitled "White Trash Nation." The magazine had told Smith her picture was to represent the All American Woman. Smith might have no-

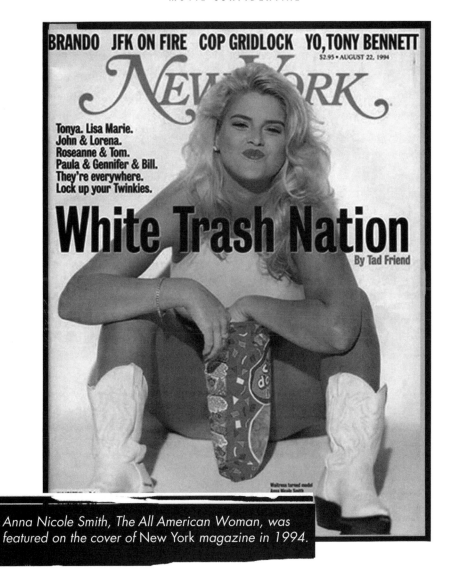

Anna Nicole Smith, The All American Woman, was featured on the cover of New York *magazine in 1994.*

ticed a red flag when the photo shoot involved her eating chips. Whatever, her attorney filed suited that the spread had damaged Smith's career. The editor of *New York* magazine, Kurt Andersen, responded, "I guess they just found the picture we chose unflattering."

In 1994 Anna Nicole Smith was still keeping tabs with a mega-rich oil tycoon named James Howard Marshall II from her stripping days. Marshall was enamored with the sex symbol, and Anna Nicole—well, many thought she was enamored with his wealth. Regardless of what the two saw in each other, or hoped to gain, they wed on June 27, 1994. Anna Nicole was twenty-six. James Howard Marshall was eighty-nine. For those of you who can't do math in your head quickly, Marshall was sixty-three years older than Smith. Let's look at it from this angle: When Marshall was sixty-three years old, the "love of his life" was just being squirted out.

Even if James Howard Marshall II were still capable of producing sperm at the over-ripe age of eighty-nine, there wasn't a lot of time to sow his seed into his silicone bride. Marshall died thirteen months into their marriage. While he lay dying, nurses said Anna Nicole would visit him, asking if Marshall wanted to see her "rosebuds." And by "rosebuds" she meant tits.

James Howard Marshall II died August 4, 1994. Anna Nicole looked forward to collecting the inheritance that is normally due to a surviving spouse. Marshall's son, Everett Pierce Marshall, called foul in an attempt to stop the widow from collecting a dime. Anna Nicole claimed when she married her elderly suitor she was told she would inherit a portion of his riches. Everett Pierce disagreed and viewed his stepmother as a gold-digging vulture. The dispute went to court, where Anna Nicole's lawyer and friend, Howard K. Stern (who later become "husband" number three), said, "E. Pierce should just pay the money he owes, mind his own business, and let Anna Nicole move on with her life."

How did the dispute go from complaint to court issue? Anna Nicole was never added to Howard Marshall's will. There was a question whether he ever intended to leave money behind for her. If so, wouldn't he have made this update instead of just stating it orally, which couldn't be proven? The battle between the two parties went on for years. Sometimes in Marshall's favor. Other times in Smith's. But how far out of control could this get? All the way to the Supreme Court, baby!

On May 1, 2006 the Supreme Court ruled in Anna Nicole Smith's favor. Everett Marshall replied by dying on June 20, 2006. Perhaps the shock was too much to handle. Anna Nicole appeared to have won, and her major obstacle was now out of the way. She celebrated the only way she knew how: She had a child on September 7, 2006 with another magnet for controversy, a man known as Larry "I'll sue ya" Birkhead.

Life was looking great though the sense of victory would be fleeting. On September 10, 2006 Anna Nicole's son, Daniel Smith, died from what would eventually be determined as an accidental overdose of methadone and antidepressants. On September 28, 2006 Smith held a "commitment ceremony" with her long-time friend and attorney, Howard K. Stern. So they were "married" but "not married." Then on February 8, 2007, not even a year after the birth of her daughter, the death of her son, the commitment to Stern, and the win at the Supreme Court, Smith was discovered dead in a hotel room from an accidental overdose of prescription medicine. Sleeping pills were said to be the major factor.

In the days after her death, the call to 911 placed by hotel staff was released to the media. A hotel employee is heard saying, "We need assistance to Room 607 at the Hard Rock. It's in reference to a white female. She's not breathing and not responsive . . . actually, it's Anna Nicole Smith." Way to name-drop!

If you're still curious to see what kind of caliber an actor Anna Nicole Smith was, check out the 1997 action movie *Skyscraper.* Many critics have referred to it as nothing more than soft-core porn. That may be unfair to the standards of soft-core porn.

29

When Should You Talk to Your Children About Sex . . . with Rob Lowe?

⚥

THE '80S BROUGHT WAVE AFTER WAVE OF movies about teenage rebellion. As part of the "Brat Pack," Rob Lowe was royalty in movies that were trying to relate to teenagers. After having acted for years, Lowe made his first huge splash in Francis Ford Coppola's *The Outsiders* (1983). Lowe played one of the Curtis brothers in a story about young men who don't fit into society.

The Outsiders is thought of as the first Brat Pack movie, with *Betsy's Wedding* being the last in 1990. In those seven years, twelve Brat Pack movies were made. Rob Lowe appeared in five of them, tying for most roles in a Brat Pack movie with Molly Ringwald and Ally Sheedy. Even outside of his famous Hollywood clique, Lowe had no problems finding work. He was everything from a hockey hero in *Youngblood* (1986) to a bum serving jury duty who finds his first love on trial for murder in *Illegally Yours* 1988. Was he one of the greatest actors of our time? No, but he had charm and he had skills and he made people want to watch movies.

Rob Lowe and his wife found themselves at the heart of a scandal involving their two nannies in 2009.

The funny thing about Rob Lowe making a movie called *Illegally Yours* is he made a private movie that could have also been called *Illegally Yours*. While at the 1988 Democratic National Convention, where the actor was showing support for Michael Dukakis, Lowe met two women at a club during an after party. After a few drinks and some schmoozing, Lowe invites the two women back to his hotel room. There the three retire to the bedroom where a video camera faces the bed and is switched from it's off position to record. The first celebrity sex tape was born that night.

As often happens when celebrities record themselves having sex, the tape was eventually leaked to the public. It may have been an awkward moment for Lowe having to explain the origins of the video in interviews. But no one could possibly be

no one could possibly be surprised by the Brat Pack

surprised by the Brat Pack member having sex with two women at once—that is until it was discovered that one of the girls was only sixteen years old.

Lowe was beginning to carry the reputation of a "Lowe" life, and to add further embarrassment, the leaked sex tape also included Lowe having sex with a friend named Justin Moritt and an aspiring model in a Paris hotel room. Rob Lowe was going to have to eat one serious shit sandwich if he wanted to maintain any chance of being a movie star.

The first ray of hope came when it was learned that the sixteen-year-old girl in question had lied about her age and used a fake ID to enter the club. Because of this, the district attorney chose not to charge Lowe with taping a sexual act with a minor.

Lowe then managed to settle with the girl's mother out of court and agreed to twenty hours of community service. Lastly, Lowe checked himself into rehab for alcohol dependency and sexual addiction.

If you can't beat 'em join 'em.

Lowe decided that to get the incident behind him, he would have to face it head on. He began making cracks about his own poor judgment and hosted an episode of *Saturday Night Live* where he was the butt of numerous jokes. And though there was a period where his career waned, he did catch a different wave to success again. Rob Lowe became part of the main cast of a television show called *The West Wing*. He had proven himself to be a viable commodity. He's been working fairly equally in television and movies since 1991 in a variety of roles. It sure looked like the '80s icon came out clean on the other side.

Life was going well. Work was steady. Lowe was now a mar-

member having sex with two women at once

ried man with two children, and anytime his name was mentioned it was in connection to his work. Then the drama train came around the corner again. Rob Lowe had fired the household chef who he accused of having sex in his bed while Lowe was out of town, stealing prescription medicines, and spreading rumors about his wife's attitude and home keeping skills. Outside of firing the suspicious chef, the doors to what the media would refer to as "nanny gate" were about to come off their hinges.

What's important here is that a week before either nanny filed their claim, the Lowes had already filed a complaint of their own. The Lowes were suing for breaching the confidentiality clause in the contracts that Laura Boyce and Jessica Gibson's signed in order to work for the family. The Lowe family stated the nannies were fired for speaking about their personal lives. Boyce claimed the contract violated her right to free speech and tried to have the charge thrown out. The judge denied her request and the charge stayed.

Jessica Gibson, the other nanny to the Lowe family, was filing charges against Lowe for sexual harassment. She claimed to have had a sexual affair with Rob Lowe and was then fired. Mr. Lowe claimed the affair was a lie Gibson was using in an attempt to blackmail him for $1.5 million.

Gibson claimed she was asked how big her boyfriend's penis was (among other other unpleasantries) and claims that the Lowes would walk around naked. After much mudslinging, all involved dropped their lawsuits. Game over. No other information was released to the public. Were the nannies paid off? Did they all agree to stop before the legal fees became too much? Was there an inner spiritual realization of peace and acceptance during a group LSD trip? Well, guess we'll never know.

30

"I'm Insane!" Christian Slater is Freaking Out!

෨ ඥ

CHRISTIAN SLATER WAS NINETEEN YEARS old when *Heathers* was released and made him a teen sensation. Slater played the bad kid. He was like the devil sitting on Winona Ryder's shoulder saying, "Why wouldn't you kill them?" Slater held on to the tough guy image, playing a skateboarder trying to solve his brother's murder in 1989's *Gleaming the Cube*. By 1990 he might have been worried about being typecast when he played a rebel hosting an illegal radio station in *Pump Up the Volume*.

Maybe he was being typecast. Or maybe the parts he played began having an affect on his personality. He was the real-life rebel that girls seemed to fawn over. In 1989 Slater was arrested for driving drunk but not before he led police on a car chase. The chase ended with Slater crashing his car into a telephone pole and kicking a cop. In 1994 he was arrested for attempting to carry a pistol onto a plane. In 1997 Christian Slater became more violent and less stable. Filming had completed for Slater's latest movie, *Hard Rain*. Slater says he doesn't remember much from the cast party, but the other guests had no problem remembering. The actor reportedly began attacking his date, punching her in the face. One of the male attendees tried to separate the two. Slater bit him on the chest. By the time police had shown up, Slater had kicked another man in the stomach. Police arrested Slater but not before he attempted to remove the officer's gun from its holster.

"I'm **insane.** *No doubt about it."*

For his violent outburst, Christian Slater was sentenced to ninety days in jail. He was released early for good behavior. Slater admitted he had been under the influence of cocaine and heroin at the time of his arrest. Once released, he told the awaiting press, "I haven't shown any great character doing drugs and alcohol. The cat's out of the bag on me, okay. I'm insane. No doubt about it."

After the controversy, he was still able to find work but never achieved the level of success he once had. On May 31, 2005 Christian Slater was in trouble again. This time he was arrested in Manhattan for sexually harassing a woman on the street. He was said to be intoxicated at that time. Cameras were present when the police arrested him. He told the reporters, "I didn't do anything," as he was placed under custody. At least he feels compelled to entertain us one way or another.

31

Olive Thomas: The Flapper Hits the Crapper

OLIVE THOMAS WAS A SEXY STARLET DUR-ing the early years of film. Her biggest role was Ginger King in *The Flapper* (1920). Like many who find their way to Hollywood, Olive did not have an easy life, and fame turned out to not be the lifesaver she hoped it would. Olive met and eventually married a fellow actor named Jack Pickford, who was the brother of the famous Mary Pickford. Their marriage could be described as rocky at best. Jack's love for the company of other women and Olive's habit for the drink made their relationship a tumultuous one.

In August of 1920, the two left for Paris on a second honeymoon in an attempt to save their marriage. After a night of celebrating, the couple returned to their hotel room at the Ritz.

Like many who find their way to Hollywood, Olive did not have an

Olive Thomas

Later, during the early hours of the morning, Jack called the front desk and said his wife needed a doctor. According to Jack Pickford, his wife was unable to sleep and had accidentally taken his mercury bichloride, used to treat syphilis, thinking it was medication for sleep. The mercury bichloride was literally eating away at Olive Thomas from the inside out. She was taken to the hospital, where she died four days later.

easy life, and fame turned out to not be the lifesaver she hoped it would.

Though her death was ruled an accidental overdose, many suspected much more sinister scenarios. Some believed Jack poisoned his wife to be done with her. The marriage was failing and he wanted out. Others felt Olive had committed suicide over discovering the shame of her husband's sexually transmitted disease. A variation of this belief is that Olive had also contracted syphilis from her husband and decided to take her own life.

After Olive's death, Jack Pickford married again twice. He died in 1933 from the effects caused by syphilis.

32

Winona Ryder and the Five-Finger Discount

ℰℛ

WHEN TIMOTHY LEARY IS YOUR GODFATHER and your parents hang out with Allen Ginsberg, no one will be surprised by the occasional odd antic. But Winona Ryder, with gorgeous girl-next-door looks, surprised many when she was arrested for shoplifting. The shoplifting charge would be the first in a row of strange allegations.

Born Winona Horowitz on October 29, 1971, she was named after the town she was born in, Winona, Minnesota. Often bullied at school, Winona was enrolled into her first acting class at the age of ten to help boost her self esteem. At the age of thirteen she was cast in the romantic comedy *Lucas* (1986) alongside Charlie Sheen and Corey Haim. It was at this point she changed her last name from Horowitz to Ryder to create her stage name. The inspiration came from her father's favorite band, Mitch Ryder and the Detroit Wheels.

Work began rolling in hard and fast once young Winona proved her abilities on the screen. In 1988 she starred in two different movies that are still loved by fans today. In *Beetle Juice* she played a goth heroine firing off quip after quip at her yuppie parents. In *Heathers*, Ryder and Christian Slater become social vigilantes, taking out their high school's clique of ultra popular students. In 1989 she played the child bride of Jerry Lee Lewis, played by Dennis Quaid, in *Great Balls of Fire*. Then in 1990 she starred along side her real-life boyfriend, Johnny Depp, in her second Tim Burton movie, *Edward Scissorhands*. Depp showed his love for Ryder by having "Winona Forever" tattooed on his arm. Guess how that worked out.

The hits kept on rolling for Winona, who was nominated for two Academy Awards. In 1993 she was nominated for Best Actress in a Supporting Role for *The Age of Innocence*. The other nomination was for the big one, Best Actress in a Leading Role, for playing Jo March in 1994's *Little Women*. Her connection to *Little Women* was a special one. In 1993 a twelve-year-old girl named Polly Klaas was abducted in Petaluma, the same town Ryder grew up in. Ryder felt a personal connection to the event and put up $200,000 of her own money as a reward for the child's safe return. On November 30, the man who abducted Klaas was arrested, and he soon admitted to murdering her. In the aftermath of Polly Klaas's abduction and murder, Winona

Ryder agreed to star in the film adaptation of *Little Women*. The book, *Little Women*, had been a favorite of Klaas, and Ryder dedicated the film to her.

Such a skyrocketing success was a blessing, but it also was a strain on Winona emotionally and physically. In 1990 she had an opportunity to act in *The Godfather: Part 3* but had to bow out—some say due to illness. She had just filmed three movies in a row—*Welcome Home, Roxy Carmichael*; *Edward Scissorhands*; and *Mermaids*. Others say pressure from her rocky romance with Johnny Depp caused her to pass. Her relationship with Depp ended and Winona sought psychiatric treatment for depression and insomnia. Depp had his tattoo altered to read "Wino Forever."

In 1997, the same year *People* magazine named her one the Fifty Most Beautiful People in the World, Winona was injured while filming the sci-fi horror more *Alien 4: Resurrection*. After being seen by a doctor, she was released back to work and given a prescription for painkillers. Winona had also injured her knee on the set of *Girl, Interrupted* (1999). In 2000 she received a star on the Hollywood walk of fame. It would be the last bit of good luck she'd have for a while.

In August of 2001, Ryder had dropped out of another movie, *Lilly and the Secret Planting*, complaining of chronic stomach pain. Unbeknownst to her, the doctor she had been referred to was under investigation for over-prescribing narcotics to his patients. He had written a prescription for an opiate-based painkiller and Valium for Ryder. What could possibly go wrong?

Three months later, in Beverly Hills, Winona Ryder was wearing the bracelets that no wants to wear. She had been arrested for shoplifting over $5,000 worth of clothing and accessories from trendy department store Saks Fifth Avenue. While detained, she was found to have pharmaceutical drugs without a prescription. Ryder had also brought into the store scissors to remove anti-theft devices and paper to wrap the stolen goods.